D1057236

Related Titles

Essay Writing Step-by-Step: A Newsweek Education Program Guide for Teens

Frankenstein: A Kaplan SAT Score-Raising Classic

The Ring of McAllister: A Score-Raising Mystery, Featuring
1,046 Must-Know SAT Vocabulary Words

SHAKING HANDS

WITH

SHAKESPEARE

by

Allison Wedell Schumacher, M.F.A.

Simon & Schuster

NEW YORK · LONDON · SYDNEY · TORONTO

Kaplan Publishing
Published by Simon & Schuster
1230 Avenue of the Americas
New York, NY 10020

For bulk sales to schools, colleges, and universities, please contact Order Department, Simon & Schuster, 100 Front Street, Riverside, NJ 08075. Phone: 1-800-223-2336. Fax: 1-800-943-9831.

Executive Editor: Jennifer Farthing
Senior Managing Editor: Eileen Mager
Production Manager: Michael Shevlin
Interior Page Design: David Chipps
Interior Page Layout: Jan Gladish

Manufactured in the United States of America
Published simultaneously in Canada

September 2004
10 9 8 7 6 5 4 3 2 1

ISBN 0-7432-4683-7

TABLE OF CONTENTS

Dedication

This book is dedicated to
Amy Vira Hettler McIlroy
and to the memory of
Donald Douglas McIlroy (1916–2004):
Lifelong educators and learners,
Shakespeare fans,
and beloved grandparents.

"My goodwill is great, though the gift small."
Pericles, Act III, Scene iv, Line 17

Acknowledgments

For their research, readership, advice, and support throughout all incarnations of this book, I owe a debt of gratitude to the following people:

Dr. Douglas B. Reeves, President, Center for Performance Assessment; Maureen McMahon, Eileen Mager, Jennifer Farthing, and Ruth Baygell at Simon and Schuster; Stephanie Shine, Artistic Director, Seattle Shakespeare Company; Alan Bryce, Artistic Director, CenterStage Theatre; Pam Eatmon, McCormick Junior High School, Cheyenne, Wyoming; Father James Schumacher of Laramie, Wyoming; Brynne Pederson Garman, Jayne Ross, and Maya Sugarman of Seattle; Jennifer Hendrickson of Los Angeles; Randi Grundahl, Jennifer Maren, and Andréa Wollenberg of Minneapolis; my wonderful family, Maïda, Eric, and Carl Wedell; and my husband, Dan Schumacher. Thank you all.

ABOUT THE AUTHOR

Allison Wedell Schumacher is an actress and lifelong Shakespeare devotee. Originally from Cheyenne, Wyoming, her love of theatre originated in the seats of the local community theatre, the Cheyenne Little Theatre Players, where her parents bought season tickets every year. She went on to earn a BA in English and Theatre from St. Olaf College in Northfield, Minnesota, where she developed a fascination with Shakespeare's language while learning about scansion in an acting class. She completed an MFA in Theatre Arts at the University of Louisville in Kentucky, where she began teaching acting and wrote her master's thesis on playing the role of Isabella in Shakespeare's *Measure for Measure*. She currently resides in Seattle, Washington, where she works steadily as an actress and writer.

Section One

❦

MEETING SHAKESPEARE: HISTORY AND LANGUAGE

SHAKESPEARE, HIS THEATRE, AND HIS TIMES: A QUICK OVERVIEW

'Tis a chronicle of day by day.
—*The Tempest*, ACT V, SCENE 1, LINE 191

JUST THE FACTS, MA'AM

Think about all the things we know about famous people these days. For instance, take the Hollywood filmmaker Steven Spielberg. Of course, you already know what he does for a living. But how hard would it be to find out where and when he was born? Or find out how many kids he has, and what their names are? Easy, right?

Believe it or not, those basic facts are pretty much all we know about the life of the famous 16th-century English playwright, William Shakespeare.

If you really wanted to, you could delve deeper into Spielberg's life and background just by doing a little bit of research on the Internet or by watching tapes of the many interviews he's done over the years. In addition to all of the things mentioned above, you could readily find out other intimate details such as how he got his start, what kinds of things inspire his work, etc.

But with Shakespeare, we don't have that option. In fact, we don't know very much about him at all. Here are all the things we know for certain:

BAPTISM: William Shakespeare was baptized at Holy Trinity Church in Stratford-upon-Avon (named so because the town of Stratford sits on the Avon River), England, on April 26, 1564.

HOUSE: Shakespeare bought a big house called New Place in Stratford in 1597. Although he lived in London off and on for the rest of his life, he never sold New Place, and his family most likely lived there full-time.

MARRIAGE: On November 28, 1582, Shakespeare was issued a marriage license allowing him to marry Anne Hathaway. He was eighteen and she was twenty-six. She was also pregnant with their first child.

CHILDREN: Shakespeare and his wife had three children. Susanna was born in 1583, and their twins, Hamnet and Judith, were born in 1585. Hamnet died in 1596, when he was only 11 years old.

BUSINESS: Along with other players, or actors, Shakespeare formed a theatre company called the Lord Chamberlain's Men in 1594 and became an owner of the Globe Theatre in 1599. He bought quite a bit of land in the Stratford area and invested in a house in London. He once testified in a court case in London.

WILL: In early 1616, Shakespeare wrote his will, leaving his "second-best bed" to his wife (no one knows why, nor what happened to his very best bed), some money and other items to his daughter Judith, and most of the rest of his estate to his daughter Susanna and her husband. He also left some money to three of the actors in his company: Richard Burbage, John Heminge, and Henry Condell.

DEATH: Shakespeare died on April 23, 1616, and was buried near the chancel of Holy Trinity Church, where he had been baptized.

BARD

A poet and singer who composes and performs songs or poems recounting the deeds of famous heroes; a master storyteller. As a proper noun, Bard has come to refer specifically to William Shakespeare as a shorter term for "the Bard of Avon."

Not much, is it? All the things we know about the man otherwise known as the *Bard* of Avon are kind of boring. It would be much more interesting if we knew more personal details. Did he write his plays at home or at a pub over a pint of ale? How did he become interested in theatre in the first place? Is there any connection between the grief over the death of his son Hamnet and the creation of the sad and tortured character Hamlet five or six years later?

Connecting the Dots

Unfortunately, we will have to be content with those basic facts. Based on those facts, however, and upon inferences derived from his plays and sonnets, many people have made educated guesses about Shakespeare's life. While these are informed decisions based on extensive research of the period in which he lived, they are really only conjecture. Here are some of the speculations that Shakespearean scholars and biographers have made about his life:

BIRTH: We do not know his exact birth date, but babies in **Elizabethan** England were usually baptized only days after their birth, so scholars have generally agreed that his date of birth was April 23. Probably the most compelling reason for this decision, however, is that he died on April 23. He could have been born as late as the 25th or as early as the 19th, but it just seems more poetic to suppose that he died on his birthday.

HOBBIES: Many people think Shakespeare had an interest in *falconry* because a falcon appears on his family's *coat of arms* and because there are numerous references to the sport in his plays.

SCHOOL: The grammar school (or elementary school) in Stratford was called the King's New School. Since William Shakespeare's father John was mayor of Stratford at the time, Shakespeare would have qualified to attend school there. There are no student records or class lists, so we have no way of knowing if he actually went there. Keep in mind, though, that most people in Shakespeare's time (including Shakespeare's own father) could not read or write, so Shakespeare had to have gone to school somewhere in order to become not only literate, but eventually a great playwright, too. Another clue: Shakespeare's work contains numerous references to books that were only

ELIZABETHAN

Anything from or relating to the time when Elizabeth I was the queen of England; specifically, the time period in England between 1558 and 1603.

FALCONRY

The practice of breeding and training hawks and other birds of prey to hunt small animals and return to the owner.

COAT OF ARMS

An emblem or picture denoting a specific family, handed down through the generations. The colors and objects used often have specific symbolism, such as a lion for courage or blue for loyalty. The phrase originally comes from the fact that a knight would wear a coat over his chain mail, and the coat was embroidered with the symbols describing the types of weapons ("arms") his family used.

printed in Latin, and at the time, grammar schools taught as much Latin as they did English. The King's New School seems like the most logical place where Shakespeare might have received his education.

TRAVEL: The general agreement is that Shakespeare never left England, because, although many of his plays take place in distant lands (Denmark, Rome, Venice, etc.), his geography is generally pretty far off the mark. For instance, his characters may travel from one place to another in a day when, in reality, it would have taken three days, and he would set cities by the sea which are actually landlocked. On the other hand, many writers bend the truth to suit their purposes when writing fiction. It is possible that Shakespeare went to some or all of the places he wrote about and simply chose to change them.

Small Group ACTivity

Imagine that you are writing a short biography of a historical person, but that you have very limited information on that person. In fact, the only things you know about that person are the following:

- His name was Jonathan Sumner.
- He was born on November 14, 1922 in Atlanta, Georgia.
- He attended Washington University in St. Louis.
- He married Jane Galbraith on March 22, 1944.
- He had three children: Katherine, Michael, and Walter.
- He moved to Los Angeles, California in 1950 and rented a house there.
- He wrote three books about the U.S. Civil War under a different name.
- He died in Los Angeles on November 18, 1970 and is buried there.

Based on this information, write a short (one- or two-page) biography of Jonathan Sumner, filling in the gaps for information you don't know based on what you think would be likely. When you're finished, compare your short biography of Jonathan Sumner with those of your friends. What information is different? Were any of your conjectures the same? What were your friends' reasons for filling in the gaps the way they did?

Classroom ACTivity

How much do you think Shakespeare drew upon his own experiences and personality when writing his plays? Many authors, such as Ernest Hemingway, use a lot of autobiographical material when writing fiction. But other authors create characters and situations they could never have known. Just because some of Shakespeare's characters were mistrustful of religion or liked wine, does that mean he felt the same way?

Organize two groups for a debate. One group argues that Shakespeare's plays are autobiographical, using specific examples. The other group argues that the man and his art are two completely different things.

SHAKESPEARE THE PLAYWRIGHT

Most scholars think that Shakespeare was an actor before he was a playwright. Once he started writing, however, his plays consumed much of his time. If you were a playwright in Elizabethan England, you would either be associated with a specific theatre company, like Shakespeare was, or you would be a freelance playwright. You might have a little more artistic freedom as a freelance playwright, but with a company, you would have a more dependable paycheck. If you belonged to a company who depended on your work for their livelihood, you would probably have a contract with the company that stated how many plays you had to write per year and how much you would get paid for each of them. This would mean that you would have to deliver your manuscripts on time so that the actors would have something to show to the public when the time came. For most of your career, you would need to write two plays per year, like Shakespeare did.

One advantage to belonging to a single company for his entire career was that Shakespeare got to know the actors really well and could tailor characters to their specific skills. Most actors tended to play one character type. Types would include kings, clowns, or **ingénues**, for instance, and so if Shakespeare were writing a play with a king in it, he would keep in mind the actor in his company who most often played kings. As a result, a relationship was formed that was beneficial to all: Shakespeare had good

> **INGÉNUE**
>
> A character type in dramatic literature. An ingénue is an innocent, naïve girl or young woman, such as Juliet in *Romeo and Juliet* or Ophelia in *Hamlet*.

actors to provide him with inspiration and character development, and in return, the actors achieved fame by skillfully portraying roles that were designed just for them.

Solo ACTivity

Pretend you are Shakespeare, writing plays or movie scripts for today's actors. Which of today's stars could be depended upon to successfully play a certain character type (clown, king, villain, ingénue, etc.)? If necessary, consult chapter four, "Shakespeare's Characters." List at least three of each, then decide which combinations of actors would work best together.

MASTER OF REVELS

A government officer appointed by Queen Elizabeth whose responsibilities were to oversee and regulate the business of theatre companies. These duties included the censorship and licensing of all plays, the arrangements for theatre companies to perform at court for the Queen, and the approval of theatre companies to be formed and to perform regularly.

Once Shakespeare finished writing a play, it had to be approved by a government official called the *Master of Revels,* who was a censor. Elizabethan England did not have the freedom of speech that we enjoy today, and so part of the Master of Revels' job was to take out all the parts that might express moral, religious, or political opinions that he felt the public should not hear. The Master of Revels then gave the playwright permission to produce the play publicly; this was called licensing.

Classroom ACTivity

What does it take to become a playwright, actor, or director today? We know that Shakespeare probably never went to college. If he had lived in the 21st century, would he have made it as a playwright? To learn about what kind of backgrounds today's actors, directors, and playwrights require, invite one of them to your class to discuss his or her education, training, and experience. Where did they go to school and for how long? Did they always want to have a career in the theatre? Where do they get their inspiration? If no such artists live in your area, try writing a letter to an actor, director, or playwright you admire.

Sides

If the play was written by hand, and there was only one copy of it, how did all the players learn their lines? Once the play was censored and licensed, the script was given to a member of the theatre company called the *prompter*. The prompter would take the only existing copy of the play and, instead of writing out an entire copy for every member of the cast, he would give each cast member a small booklet or scroll called a *side*, which contained only that character's lines and cues. It was a cheaper and more efficient way to make sure everyone learned his lines: First, paper and ink were expensive, and second, there was no such thing as a copy machine, so all copying had to be done by hand. There were printing presses, but having a script printed out just for the players would have been an unnecessarily expensive and time-consuming undertaking. To ensure that the actor would know when to say each line, his side might also contain cues or prompts, which would be the last few words of the line that came before it.

PROMPTER

The person in an Elizabethan theatre company who was in charge of making sure all actors had their scripts or sides and who would aid in rehearsals by following the script and providing words if actors forgot their lines. The prompter was also in charge of running performances (similar to a modern-day stage manager) and of keeping track of which costumes, props, and music were needed for each play.

SIDE

A booklet or scroll containing a single character's cues ("prompts") and lines from a play.

What do sides look like? In the left-hand box on the following page, you will see part of a scene from Act III, Scene i of *Hamlet* the way it is printed in a script today. In the right-hand box, you will see the same scene, containing only the lines and cues that would be in a side given to the actor playing Hamlet in Shakespeare's company.

You can see that there aren't nearly as many words on the right as there are on the left. It would definitely take much less time, paper, and effort to copy a play by hand using the method on the right than to copy the entire play for each actor.

Hamlet Today	Elizabethan Side for Hamlet
OPHELIA: Good my lord, how does your honour for this many a day?	**OPHELIA:** ...for this many a day?
HAMLET: I humbly thank you: well, well, well.	**HAMLET:** I humbly thank you: well, well, well.
OPHELIA: My lord, I have remembrances of yours, that I have longed long to re-deliver; I pray you, now receive them.	**OPHELIA:** ...now receive them.
HAMLET: No, not I; I never gave you aught.	**HAMLET:** No, not I; I never gave you aught.
OPHELIA: My honour'd lord, you know right well you did, and with them words of so sweet breath composed as made the things more rich; their perfume lost, take these again; for to the noble mind rich gifts wax poor when givers prove unkind. There, my lord.	**OPHELIA:** ...There, my lord.
HAMLET: Ha, Ha! Are you honest?	**HAMLET:** Ha, Ha! Are you honest?
OPHELIA: My lord?	**OPHELIA:** My lord?
HAMLET: Are you fair?	**HAMLET:** Are you fair?
OPHELIA: What means your lordship?	**OPHELIA:** What means your lordship?
HAMLET: That if you be honest and fair, your honesty should admit no discourse to your beauty.	**HAMLET:** That if you be honest and fair, your honesty should admit no discourse to your beauty.

Small Group ACTivity

With a partner, choose any two-person scene from a Shakespeare play. Decide which character you will play, then hand-write your own sides from the script. Remember, a side consists of only your lines, with a few words from the end of your partner's lines to prompt you. Act out the scene using your sides, then act out the scene using regular scripts. Discuss which one was easier and why.

Sources

Shakespeare got ideas for plots and stories from a lot of different places. In Elizabethan England, there were no copyright laws, so copying other people's work or using it without permission was a pretty common practice. Shakespeare borrowed plots, situations, and characters from many different sources, including history, mythology, legend, fiction, other plays, and the Bible. Sometimes he used several different sources and wove them all into one play. Of course, he changed what he wanted or needed to change, making the stories uniquely his own, and yet Elizabethan audiences were happy to see characters and stories they recognized. We'll discuss specific sources for plays in chapter three.

SHAKESPEARE'S TIMES: ELIZABETHAN ENGLAND

There were a lot of changes going on in England during Shakespeare's lifetime. England was finally establishing itself as a major European power and was enjoying great cultural and economic advances. Perhaps the biggest change of all, though, was the fact that England had a female ruler, Queen Elizabeth. She was born in 1533, and became the queen in 1558, which means she had already been ruling England for six years by the time Shakespeare was born. Kings and queens of England were said to rule by *divine right*. In other words, people believed that the royal bloodline had been anointed by God to be the ruling family of England. However, many people thought Queen Elizabeth should get married so that they could have a proper king. But Elizabeth knew that if

DIVINE RIGHT

The belief that a monarch's right to rule a nation comes directly from God, rather than from the people they rule. This stands in stark contrast to the democratic system of government, in which people can only gain leadership positions by being elected to them by the people they intend to lead.

11

CHAIN OF BEING

The order in which Elizabethans pictured the universe, beginning at the top with God and ending with the smallest and most insignificant things. The human part of the chain was also in a very specific order, with the Queen at the top and beggars and slaves at the bottom. Everyone in between was categorized according to the social and economic standing of the family they were born into, and it was considered going against creation and God himself to try to break out of one's place in the chain.

PROTESTANT

A person or church that is Christian but not Catholic and who denies that the Pope has authority over all Christians. Also, Protestants believe they can be forgiven for their sins without the aid of a priest (or member of the clergy). The Protestant Church was formed in the mid-1500s and was solidified as the Church of England during Queen Elizabeth I's reign.

CATHOLIC

Before the 16th century, the Catholic Church was the only Christian church. It emphasizes the sacraments (such as baptism, marriage, and communion), tradition, ordained clergy (such as priests) and good works of piety and charity.

she did marry, she would be giving up most of her power to her husband, and so she chose instead to remain "The Virgin Queen."

The English people believed in what they called a *Chain of Being*: Everything in the universe belonged in one long chain, organized in order of importance. God was at the top of this chain, of course, followed by Queen Elizabeth, the nobility, priests, and bishops of the church, gentlemen (people with titles), commoners, beggars, and slaves. No matter where they were on the chain, men were thought to be superior to women. So, you can see why people found it difficult to accept the concept of having a queen ruling over them, rather than a king.

As a result, Queen Elizabeth had a lot to prove. She had to show that she was just as good at running the empire as any man. In 1588, the English Navy defeated the Spanish Armada, a group of warships sent by King Philip II of Spain, who thought that Elizabeth should not be on the throne because she was female and because she had chosen to be *Protestant* rather than *Catholic*. Because of this great and rather unexpected defeat, the English finally felt that they had established themselves as a military power. And even though Queen Elizabeth herself had very little to do with the actual battle plans, the English Navy's victory helped boost her popularity with her subjects.

In fact, Elizabeth turned out to be a very successful queen. When she became queen, England was heavily in debt and was torn by political and religious disagreements. It had a weak military and was at the whim of its two major enemies, France and Spain. Plus, England was a very uneducated and poor nation. But Elizabeth made a lot of improvements. She supported commerce and trade, bringing England out of debt and raising the standard of living. She brought her people together in common support of her. She made England into a strong military force, and supported the efforts of historians and of explorers such as Sir Walter Raleigh, who founded the colony of Virginia in America and named it after Elizabeth, his Virgin Queen. She supported education, founding colleges and making sure most towns had elementary schools. Indeed, Queen Elizabeth's reign was unusually long and prosperous.

Elizabethan Beliefs

Religion

Although Elizabethan England was a very religious society, non-religious ways of thinking were becoming more prevalent in England than ever before. On the one hand, Elizabethans were deeply religious, and believed that everything they did in their daily lives on earth would determine whether they went to heaven or hell. They were required by law to attend church every Sunday and to take communion three times a year, or they would have to pay a fine. (It was not long before this that people had believed that it was a sin to study anything, such as science, that did not have to do with Christianity.)

But at the same time, a movement called *humanism* was gaining acceptance. Humanists felt that learning about classical studies (the writings of the ancient Greeks and Romans) could be as worthy a pursuit as the study of the Bible. In other words, they felt that goodness and knowledge could come from human beings without the aid of a divine being. Even though they may not have consciously defined their beliefs this way, many Elizabethans believed in both Christianity and humanism at the same time, although they might seem contradictory.

HUMANISM

A cultural system of beliefs based on the idea that good things come from people rather than (or in addition to) any supernatural deity; in Elizabethan times, this meant a return to the study of ancient Greek and Roman writings and philosophy rather than the study of the Bible or other religious texts.

There was no longer just one type of Christian, either, and this was becoming a problem. A major debate was raging between the Protestants and the Catholics.

Elizabeth's father, King Henry VIII, had broken away from Catholicism to form his own Protestant church, the Church of England. There was still a lot of controversy over this situation. Most of the rest of Europe was still Catholic, and there were many English people who believed that Henry had been wrong to leave the Catholic Church. It was not until Henry's daughter, Queen Elizabeth, came to the throne that Protestantism became the accepted form of Christian worship in England. For the most part, she managed to unite her people in support of the Church of England. Of course, there were still Catholics in England, but they had to worship in secret, because they were sometimes punished or even killed for disagreeing with the government's choice of religion.

Freedom of Speech

Although there was no freedom of speech as we know it today, writers of the time could still create dissent against the government if they did not agree with its political or religious views. Queen Elizabeth was aware of the fact that plays could sway the general public.

In fact, in 1601, one of Shakespeare's plays was used for just such a purpose. Robert Devereaux, second Earl of Essex, wanted the throne for himself, and he was pretty sure he could get it by convincing some of Queen Elizabeth's supporters to endorse him instead. So one of Essex's friends, Sir Gelli Meyrick, convinced Shakespeare and his company to perform *Richard II*. Why this particular play? *Richard II* is about a monarch whose popularity is declining and whose cousin, Henry Bolingbroke, very much wanted to be King himself. Bolingbroke manages to gain the support of most of the public and forces Richard to give up the throne to him. Because of the play's obvious parallels to the situation Elizabeth now found herself in with Essex, Meyrick thought *Richard II* would be just the thing to convince the public that they should join Essex against Queen Elizabeth. Shakespeare and his company put on the play with great reluctance, as Elizabeth had been a great supporter of Shakespeare's work and he was very grateful for it. As it turned out, Essex's uprising quickly lost steam, as most of the public remained loyal to the queen. Essex was arrested, tried, and beheaded for his trouble.

However, Queen Elizabeth wasn't taking any chances. It was because of the danger of episodes just like this that she insisted that playwrights should not be allowed to write about religious or political subjects. As a safeguard, she had the Master of Revels go through each manuscript and take out anything political or religious.

Solo ACTivity

Compare the society you live in to Elizabethan England. The left-hand column of the chart below lists some of the aspects of Elizabethan society. How does your society compare? Fill in the right-hand column for each point.

Elizabethan England	*My society*
The law requires us to worship as members of the Church of England, and we have to go to church once a week.	
God has chosen a Queen to lead our country.	
All a person has to do to become a ruler is to be born into the royal family.	
The Master of Revels can keep us from saying anything negative about the government or religion.	
If my parents are farmers, I will most likely be a farmer.	
I cannot marry anyone who is higher than I am on the social ladder.	
If my family is poor, I will never go to college.	
If I am female, I am not allowed to go to school.	
Women are considered inferior to men in all ways.	

SECULAR

Philosophy, literature, art, or music that is not religious or spiritual in nature or subject matter; having nothing to do with any spiritual deity.

Without religious subject matter, many playwrights turned to classical subjects, which meant that humanism had a chance to flourish in the Elizabethan theatre. As a result, deep and devoted religious beliefs stood side by side with an interest in *secular* subjects and pastimes in every Elizabethan's life.

Elizabethan Entertainment

Elizabethans enjoyed a wide range of entertainment. Built beside Shakespeare's theatre, the Globe, was a building called Paris Gardens. Paris Gardens was an arena where people could go to see bear- and bull-baiting. The bear or bull was chained to a wall or other immobile object, and dogs were allowed to tease and "bait" it while the spectators looked on. If the bear or bull were able to kill one of the dogs, another dog was simply released in its place. Occasionally, a blinded bear was chained up and five or six men would stand around it and whip it.

Another popular Elizabethan pastime was cockfighting, in which two roosters were made to fight to the death in a pit while observers watched and made bets as to which would win. (Clearly, "cruelty to animals" was not yet a phrase that had any meaning to the Elizabethans.)

Cockfighting and bear-baiting were the theatre's main competition for the public's attention, so theatre companies had to make sure that they delivered what the public wanted to see. This was one reason they so often contracted with playwrights, so that they would have a constant stream of new material to show their patrons.

Fortunately for the theatre companies, Queen Elizabeth very much enjoyed the theatre in general and Shakespeare's work in particular. But the Queen would never come out to the theatre among the common people to see a play. Instead, she made the theatre come to her. She would summon a company of players to her court, have her carpenters erect a stage in the great hall, and have the theatre company perform a play or two of her choosing. This usually happened during the Christmas holidays in the evening, which meant the great hall had to be lit with candles and torches (remember that the light bulb wouldn't be invented for another two hundred years or so), which was an expensive undertaking. Documentation shows that Shakespeare's theatre company—called the **Lord Chamberlain's Men** because they were financially supported by a nobleman called the Lord Chamberlain—performed for Queen Elizabeth at her court at least 32 times.

Queen Elizabeth was also a great fan and supporter of music, both secular and religious. Composers of both secular and religious music flourished under her protection. She was responsible for the rise in popularity of chamber music. Because of her, it became fashionable for those who could afford it to build a special room, or "chamber," just for music to be played in. She employed a 32-piece orchestra at her court, and began putting on free concerts to the public, so that even the poorest of her subjects could enjoy an afternoon of musical entertainment.

> **LORD CHAMBERLAIN'S MEN**
>
> The name of the theatre company that Shakespeare belonged to in London, consisting of 10 to 12 men, called so because they were financially supported by the Lord Chamberlain.

Classroom ACTivity

Imagine that you are the Master of Revels and that Queen Elizabeth has ordered you to plan an evening of entertainment for her and her guests. Divide the class into four groups, and put one group each in charge of plays, music, dancing, and poetry. Choose an evening or class period for your entertainment to take place. Once each group decides what they want to do, they may perform it themselves, play a recording of it (such as a film version of the play they have chosen or a recording of the music they have chosen), or ask someone else to perform it—for instance, if your school has a music department, perhaps you can find someone who plays the recorder or a group who sings madrigals; or, perhaps your town has an early music ensemble who would be willing to come play for the class or a dance teacher who can teach or perform early dances. As your evening of entertainment draws near, you may even wish to print up scrolls for those who will attend, listing what will be performed and who will be performing it. Then, sit back and enjoy!

Daily Life in Elizabethan England

Poverty and Plague

Although Queen Elizabeth was responsible for improving the general economy of England, the various classes seemed to get even further apart. In many cases, the rich got richer while the poor got poorer. Homeless beggars were very common, as there was no system in place to take care of them. Epidemic diseases such as the ***plague*** were still prevalent, even though the worst of the plague was over. But since the black (or bubonic) plague was a disease spread by fleas from rats, London—a dirty, crowded city—was the perfect place for it to thrive. During Shakespeare's lifetime, the plague took about 75,000 lives. Given that the total population of London was 200,000 at the time, this was a huge loss.

PLAGUE

An outbreak of infectious disease with a high death rate; in Elizabethan England, this meant the bubonic plague, which killed thousands at the turn of the 17th century.

Although the Elizabethans did not know what caused the plague or how to cure it, they did figure out that it was very contagious. As a result, the theatres were closed during times of plague. Any house where a person had died of plague was locked up for a month, and the door was painted with a red cross and the words "Lord have mercy upon us."

Because poverty was so widespread, crime was a constant danger. Pickpockets were everywhere, and people were advised not to travel at night, whether in the country or in the city. Some of the richer people hired bodyguards. When thieves and murderers were caught, the punishment was severe. Public whippings and

Small Group ACTivity

Imagine that it is possible to be elected to the office of Mayor of London in Elizabethan England, and that you are running for that position. The election is coming up soon, and you have to establish your platform and write a campaign speech. What will you promise to change? What morals and values will you promise to uphold? For instance, what will you tell the voters about Protestants, Catholics, and humanists? What will you say about the plague? In what ways will you promise to support Queen Elizabeth?

Decide on your platform and write your campaign speech. (If you design any other campaign materials, such as posters, remember that most of your voters are illiterate.) Deliver your campaign speech to your friends and family.

Classroom ACTivity

Many of Shakespeare's plays discuss issues that are considered controversial. In two teams, choose a controversial issue in a Shakespearean play you've read and hold a debate about it. For example: Is *The Merchant of Venice* a racist play? Does *Taming of the Shrew* have sexist overtones? With one team arguing yes and the other arguing no, debate the issue.

brandings were not uncommon, and executions were generally done by beheading or hanging. More minor offenders were left in the stocks (boards with holes for their heads and hands) in public squares, sometimes for days at a time, where passersby could taunt them or throw garbage at them.

Elizabethan Households

In a typical Elizabethan household there wasn't much time to relax, because all the work had to be done during daylight hours. Houses were generally small—only one or two rooms—so rooms often had more than one use. For instance, when it was time for a meal, a board was set up on supports to make a table. This is why the word "board" came to be synonymous with "meal," as in the expression "room and board." Stools were placed around the table for diners to sit, although if there were more people than stools, the adults were allowed to sit and the young children generally had to stand at the table for the meal. Most people did not bother with plates; instead, large, thick, stale pieces of bread (called "trenchers") were used. Those who could afford them did use plates, although they were square rather than round, which is how the expression "a square meal" came about. Forks were only just coming into use; instead, people used spoons or their hands.

The main dish was almost always meat, often two or three kinds. On any given day, you might see beef, veal, pork, chicken, lamb, mutton (meat from an adult sheep), rabbit, or goat served at the dinner table. The meat often had an elaborate sauce to hide the flavor, because animals were generally slaughtered in the fall and the meat barreled for use throughout the year. (You can imagine that it would not taste very good by the time spring came around!) There was the occasional vegetable, such as cabbage or turnips, and fruit, fruit pies, or cheese for dessert. The Elizabethans especially loved sweets, and chocolate (as well as the tomato) was introduced from the New World during Elizabeth's reign. Because clean, good-tasting water was scarce, adults and children alike drank beer or wine made from grapes, apples or other fruits, or honey.

Classroom ACTivity

Serve an Elizabethan feast. Serve any combination of roasted chicken legs and wings, boiled cabbage or other vegetables, fruit pies, meat pies, and cheese. Use bread trenchers for plates, and serve apple cider as the beverage. Eat with large spoons or with your hands. Soak up honey with bread from your trencher. Be creative with the desserts!

Elizabethan houses often did not have floorboards, but instead had dirt floors. To make the place smell cleaner, they would cover the floor in rushes (or "threshes") and place a board (or "threshold") at the bottom of the doorway to keep the threshes from falling out into the street.

Most houses didn't have windows in the modern sense, because glass was scarce and expensive. They did, however, place small holes, perhaps six inches square, in the wall near the ceiling, where extra smoke from the cooking fire could escape and natural light could come in. Since these holes also let in the wind, they came to be called "wind holes," or "windows."

An Elizabethan house did not have much in the way of furniture. A family would often sleep together in the same room. If they owned a bed, it was generally reserved for the adults. A bed consisted of a wooden frame with interlacing ropes across it, on top of which a hay-stuffed mattress was laid. The ropes would generally loosen over time, causing the mattress to sag, and would therefore have to be tightened periodically. Since a bed was more comfortable when the ropes were tight, the phrase "sleep tight" was coined to mean "have a good sleep."

SHAKESPEARE'S THEATRE

In Shakespeare's time, theatre was very different than it is today, beginning with the architecture. Shakespeare's Globe Theatre, for instance, was circular, with an open space in the middle. The stage was on one edge of the circle and was what is known as a **thrust**, that is, there were playgoers on three sides, as if the stage had been "thrust" out into the audience. The stage had two levels. The first level of the stage was where most of the action took place, and the second story, called the **gallery**, was used for things like balcony scenes (as in *Romeo and Juliet*) or fairy worlds (as in *A Midsummer Night's Dream*). Sometimes, musicians sat in the gallery to provide background music or sound effects, such as birdcalls and thunder. Occasionally, when the gallery was not being used by musicians or players, noblemen or other prominent people were allowed to sit there. Of course, this meant they were looking down on the actors' heads and the view was not all that good. However, being seen by everyone else was more important to them than seeing the play themselves.

THE GLOBE

THRUST

A stage surrounded by the audience on three sides; the fourth side is a wall with doors leading into the backstage area, through which actors can make their entrances and exits.

GALLERY

A balcony with a roof in an open-air theatre in which audience members may sit to watch a play.

Solo ACTivity

Create a timeline of Shakespeare's life. Using one color or set of symbols, show the significant dates in Shakespeare's life, as well as the approximate dates of each of his plays, when the Globe Theatre was erected, etc. Using a different color or set of symbols, show significant dates in the life of Elizabethan England: the defeat of the Spanish Armada, the plagues, the founding of the American colony of Virginia, and Elizabeth's death, just to name a few. Make the timeline as big as you would like, so that it is easy to read, and be as creative as you can—use magazine cutouts, draw your own pictures, or use computer graphics, for example.

Pit (or Yard)

The middle of a circular outdoor theatre such as the Globe. The pit was a flat, dirt floor on which audience members could stand to watch the play. The stage jutted out into the pit and was roughly five feet above its surface, so those standing in the pit would be looking up at the players.

Groundling

The informal Elizabethan term for those audience members at the Globe Theatre who stood in the pit to watch the play. They were called this because the floor of the pit was literally bare ground.

The rest of the circular theatre was three stories high, with benches where the audience could sit (it cost a bit more if you wanted a cushion for the wooden seat); these were called galleries. There was an open space called a *yard* or a *pit* in the middle of the circle in front of the stage, where other audience members could stand. A ticket for the seated part of the theatre cost twice as much as a ticket to stand in the yard, because patrons could sit down and be sheltered from sun and rain. As a result, the poorer theatre patrons tended to be the ones standing on the ground to watch the plays and were therefore called *groundlings*. They sometimes stood a long time, as plays lasted up to four hours. In all, the Globe could hold about 3,000 people.

Unlike other theatres, the Globe was owned by the theatre company that used it. Most theatre companies had to rent space every time they wanted to produce a play, and, as a result, they were never sure where they would be because this differed according to what space was available and what they could afford at the time. The Globe, however, was owned by several different people, including Shakespeare. They were called shareholders, and all were members of the Lord Chamberlain's Men. Having their own theatre meant that they had a permanent home in London, and no longer needed to tour their shows to make money. As their reputation grew, people knew they could go to the Globe and be assured of seeing good entertainment.

Solo ACTivity

Choose one of these two projects to work on: Draw a map of Elizabethan London showing the location of the Old Globe and other landmarks, or build a three-dimensional model of the Globe theatre. For the map, you may make it as large and detailed as you like. For the model, you may build it out of whatever material you like; just be sure to show the three tiers of gallery seating, the pit, and the location of the stage.

Costumes

One of the biggest expenses for a theatre company was costumes and props. The Elizabethan concept of costuming was different than it is today. For one thing, the Elizabethans had very little knowledge of how people dressed before their time. So, even in plays that portrayed historical subject matter (such as *Julius Caesar,* which takes place in ancient Rome, or *Henry IV,* which takes place in England in 1402–03, almost two centuries before Shakespeare wrote the play), the actors would have been dressed in contemporary Elizabethan attire instead of in *period costume.* Nonetheless, theatre companies took great care to costume their characters lavishly, and a lot of money was spent obtaining and maintaining costumes.

The actors wore what is called *court dress.* If an Elizabethan were lucky enough to be invited to the Queen's court for a visit, he would dress in the very best clothes he owned, and this type of clothing was what actors used onstage. The modern equivalent would be seeing a play with all the actors dressed in tuxedos or evening gowns.

That does not mean that all the actors looked alike on stage. Small accessories, called *props*, were used to aid in the audience's understanding of various characters. For instance, an actor playing a knight might have worn part or all of a suit of armor and carried a sword, whereas a queen might have been given a crown to wear and an elaborate, fancy chair to sit in.

PERIOD COSTUME

Costumes designed to look like what was worn in a specific period (i.e., a specific time and place in history). For instance, period costumes for the American 1960s would look like what people typically wore in America in the '60s.

COURT DRESS

The style of clothing approved for wearing at a royal court. Any monarch (kings, queens, etc.) was considered important enough that people would wear the very best and most fashionable clothes they owned in the sovereign's presence.

PROP

Short for "property," any object that is used in the performance of the play that is not painted scenery or costume. Props include everything from furniture to knickknacks to anything the characters might use, such as weapons or food.

Solo ACTivity

Be a costume designer. Imagine that you are in charge of designing costumes for a modern-day theatre company, but that they want to see drawings of costumes for both Elizabethan dress and contemporary dress.

Choose a character from any Shakespeare play, and do some research. What would this character have worn had he or she lived in Elizabethan times? Do a sketch, complete with colors, of what the costume should look like. For the contemporary costume, research fashion magazines and clothing catalogs, and think, "If this character were alive right now, what would he or she wear?" Do another color sketch of the contemporary costume.

Scenery

One thing the Elizabethan theatre did not have was scenery. Believe it or not, the concept had not really occurred to anyone—at least, not in the form we know it today. If a scene took place in a forest, it is not as if someone had painted an elaborate backdrop of trees. If a scene took place in an alehouse, there was no bar or kegs of ale. Instead, audiences knew where the action was taking place because of the dialogue, and they were expected to use their imaginations to picture the setting.

There was no shortage of special effects at the Globe Theatre, however. The stage was equipped with a trap door so that characters such as devils or ghosts could seem to disappear or rise up. There was flying apparatus so that fairies or gods could float above the stage or descend from the sky. There were special tables that made it look like a decapitated body was lying next to its severed head (there were holes in the table top for two actors—one whose head was below the surface of the table, and one whose head was above). There were musicians to provide birdcalls with flutes and thunder with drums. If blood were needed on stage, an actor would carry a sponge soaked in vinegar or other red liquid in the appropriate spot in his costume and squeeze it at just the right time during a swordfight.

Small Group ACTivity

Choose a short scene (or part of a scene) from a Shakespeare play that takes place in a specific setting: on a beach, in a tavern, in a great hall, on the castle battlements. Perform it once for your friends or family without telling them where it is, and see if they can get a sense of the setting just by watching you. Then, create as much of the scene as you possibly can: draw scenery on the blackboard or large sheets of paper, and use furniture and other props. Play the scene for your audience again and discuss the differences. Was it easier for you to act in the scene when you had a concrete environment? When your audience members could only envision the setting, did they all come up with different ideas? Did they find the scene more effective with or without scenery?

Audience

When you go to see a play today, you sit in one seat and do not move until intermission or the end of the play. When the lights go down, that is your cue to stop talking, so that you and your fellow audience members can concentrate on the action of the play. Food and drink are usually not allowed in the theatre.

When you go to see a football game today, you can get up and down from your seat as often as you want. You know the game is starting because loud music begins to play. You can discuss the action with your friends and even yell at the players on the field if you do not think that they are doing a good job. You can eat and drink as much as you want.

Believe it or not, being an audience member of the theatre in Shakespeare's time was more like going to see a modern-day football game. As mentioned before, the plays took place in the afternoon, usually starting at two o'clock. The Globe was an ***open-air theatre***, so audience members could see each other clearly, see what others were wearing and whom they had come with, wave to and chat

OPEN-AIR THEATRE

A theatre that was not enclosed, so as to let in as much natural light as possible. The stage and the galleries had roofs over them, but the center of the structure, called the pit, was open to the sky.

with their friends, etc. A trumpeter would sound several blasts on his horn to signal the start of the play. Once the play began, audience members could move freely about the yard or the galleries, discuss the action of the play amongst themselves, and yell funny quips or insults to the characters onstage. Occasionally, if they did not like the play that was being presented, they would

25

throw things, such as fruit or even wood, until they got their way. In addition, there were people moving about the crowd selling food such as apples, pears, and nuts; and even wine, ale, tobacco, and playbills were available for purchase.

All this makes it sound as though Elizabethan audiences never really paid attention when they came to see plays, which is not true. Given how many theatres there were in London at the time and how many new plays Shakespeare and his contemporaries were having to churn our per year to meet the public demand, it is clear that theatre was a popular and beloved pastime of Elizabethans, and Shakespeare was at the forefront of that trend.

Classroom ACTivity

Knowing all the distractions Elizabethan audiences had, how much of the plays do you think they really absorbed?

Choose any Shakespearean play on film and watch it as a class. Before you watch, assign various class members roles in the crowd: Some should be noblemen, sitting as close to the television screen as possible without blocking it, so they can see it and the rest of the class. A couple of students should be food vendors. The rest of the "crowd" should try to watch the play, but feel free to answer back to the characters if you feel so compelled, comment to your classmates when you find something interesting or disturbing, and get up to stretch or buy fruit if you want to.

Remember, though, that the point is to absorb as much of the play as you can. Afterward, answer questions on the plot and characters (your teacher can have these ready for you) and see how many you answer correctly. Discuss the experience with your classmates. Was it difficult to pay attention? Why or why not? Would you always like to see plays this way?

✖ CHAPTER TWO ✖

Shakespeare's Language: Say *What?*

I would be loath to cast away my speech: for besides that it is excellently well penned, I have taken great pains to con it.

—*Twelfth Night*, Act i, Scene v, Lines 170–172

TOUGH STUFF

Okay, I'll admit it: Shakespeare is hard. Hard to read, hard to understand. There are very few people in the world who can just sit down and read Shakespeare as if it were the Sunday comics. The rest of the world, myself included, finds reading Shakespeare to be a bit of a struggle—an extremely rewarding struggle, but a struggle nonetheless.

The problem: Although Shakespeare's language is very beautiful, it can be difficult to understand, especially at first. Anybody from the 21st century can still relate to Shakespeare's characters and to the situations they find themselves in; it is just that those characters talk so differently from the way we do today.

But if language is the only barrier we have to cross, we can overcome that in no time. By "overcome that," what I mean is that you will be *speaking* Shakespeare's language in no time. After all, the purpose of this book isn't to have more people sitting in rooms by themselves reading Shakespeare silently. The reason for that may surprise you: Shakespeare's plays were never meant to be read.

Huh?! I'll say it again:

SHAKESPEARE'S PLAYS WERE NEVER MEANT TO BE READ.

They were meant to be *heard.*

They were meant to be *seen.*

They were meant to be *acted.*

But they were never meant to be read. In fact, Shakespeare's plays were not even officially printed and sold as books until seven years after he died. There are two main reasons for this. First, as you know from chapter one, Elizabethan theatre companies paid playwrights for their plays. Think about it: If you spent a large amount of money to get a playwright to write a play just for your company, would you be happy if some other company was able to get the script and start performing it and making money from it? If the plays had been put into print, this would have been possible. The second reason was that most of Shakespeare's audience could not read. They were **aural** learners, meaning that they absorbed more information by listening to it. So, an Elizabethan theatergoer could see a play once and be able to repeat large passages of it word for word. By contrast, many people in our television-and-computer age today are visual learners, who learn best from images and the printed word. Shakespeare's audience had no use for plays on paper; therefore, it simply was not important to him that his plays be printed.

AURAL

Relating to the sense of hearing. An "aural learner" learns best by hearing things (rather than seeing/reading them).

In the nearly 400 years since Shakespeare died, his plays have gone from being perceived as everyday entertainment to being perceived as something that only nerdy scholars can understand. Before Shakespeare's plays were widely distributed in print, seeing and hearing them was the only way people knew them. In fact, it was not long ago in the American West that cowboys, outlaws, trappers, traders, and miners went around spouting Shakespeare. In the mining towns of gold-rush era (mid-1800's) California, going to see a Shakespeare play ranked right up there with drinking and gambling on a miner's list of favorite things to do for fun.

It was only recently that people started thinking of Shakespeare's plays as books to be studied rather than as plays to be seen and enjoyed. And because many people are now more familiar with Shakespeare's plays as long, dense books, they think a person needs to be incredibly smart to understand them. After all, when you are reading a book, you only have the words on the page to aid in your understanding, so if you don't understand those words… well, you're in trouble. But when you're seeing a play—even if you are the one putting it on—you have so many other things to help you: the nuance of the actors' voices, their facial expressions, their body language, and the costumes, props, music, and scenery. All of these rich and wonderful things come together to aid your understanding of the world Shakespeare has created for you. To enjoy that, you don't even have to know how to read! So Shakespeare is *not* just for smart people, because you do not need any formal education at all to be able to watch something and enjoy it.

Classroom ACTivity

Choose a scene from a Shakespearean play on film (consult the list in Appendix B). Divide the class into two groups. Have one group watch the scene once. Have the other group only *listen* to the scene once. Then, both groups answer questions on what they remember from the scene. Compare responses and discuss which was more difficult and why. **Scene Suggestions:** *Hamlet,* Act III, Scene iv; *Twelfth Night,* Act III, Scene i.

A DIFFERENT LANGUAGE

When you talk to your parents or your teacher, do you ever get the feeling that you are speaking a different language? Occasionally, you might let loose a couple of sentences that your friends would understand perfectly, but the adults around you simply stare at you blankly. Have you ever wondered why? Oftentimes, different generations have trouble understanding each other because of *slang*. Various slang words and expressions come into (and out of) style every few years. Sometimes slang stays around and gets added to the English language permanently, but more often than not, it simply gets forgotten.

SLANG

An informal vocabulary made up of non-standard word usage and invented words. Although sometimes slang ends up in standard English, most slang does not last very long.

For example, take the word "good." Every generation has a different slang synonym for it. Depending upon how old they are, your grandparents may have used the words "groovy" or "neat" to describe something they liked; your parents may have called a good thing "awesome" or, strangely enough, "bad." And you? Well, the words of the moment among teenagers in Seattle are "super-sweet" and "phat," but that will probably have changed by the time this book goes to press. Believe it or not, in Shakespeare's time, one of the words they used to describe a good situation was "meet." For instance, in *Measure for Measure*, Act I, Scene ii, Claudio says, "We thought it *meet* to hide our love." What he means is, "We thought it would be *best* to hide our love."

So you can see that even today, the English language is constantly changing. This is the reason many people find Shakespeare so difficult to understand.

Two Stabilizing Inventions

At the time Shakespeare was born, the English language was only a couple of centuries old; before that, most people in England spoke Latin or French. Even during Shakespeare's lifetime, most public records, such as the record of Shakespeare's baptism, were written in Latin. As a result, Shakespeare was writing in a language that was very new and had few definite rules. It was still changing rapidly. Luckily, there were a couple of inventions close to the time that Shakespeare lived that stopped the language from continuing to change so quickly. If these inventions had not come into being, we might not be able to understand Shakespeare's plays at all today.

The printing press, invented about 100 years before Shakespeare was born, made it possible for books to be produced in large quantities. Before this innovation, books had to be copied by hand, and they were therefore very rare and very expensive. As a result, language (English or otherwise) was not recorded with much permanence and therefore changed much more quickly than it does today.

The other innovation that slowed the change of language was the dictionary. One of the first English dictionaries was written by an Englishman named Samuel Johnson about 120 years after Shakespeare died. Since there was finally a written record of what words were in use and what those words meant, English words no longer changed their meaning so quickly.

If it had not been for the printing press and the dictionary, the English language might have gone on changing so rapidly that the English of the late 1500s might be unrecognizable to us today. For example, consider the famous writer Geoffrey

Chaucer, who wrote the *Canterbury Tales* in about 1387, only two centuries before Shakespeare wrote his plays. If you try to read an untranslated version of the *Canterbury Tales*, you will probably find it nearly impossible to understand. That is because Chaucer was writing in what is known as **Middle English**, which is much different from the **Modern English** that we speak today. What is really surprising, though, is that the Middle English period ended in about 1500, when the Modern English period began. So, technically speaking, Shakespeare wrote during the Modern English period, meaning that he wrote in the same type of English that you speak right now!

A Rose by Any Other Name

So although the English that Shakespeare used was slightly different than the language we speak today, it has not changed so much as to be unrecognizable. Many of the differences lie in the fact that there are words that are still in use but no longer mean the same thing as they meant in Shakespeare's time. Some of those words are listed below.

MIDDLE ENGLISH

The form of English that was spoken between about 1100 and 1500. Middle English was a combination of Old English (a Germanic language also known as Anglo Saxon), Latin, and Norse.

MODERN ENGLISH

The form of English that started about 1500 and is still spoken today. Modern English differs from Middle English mainly in vocabulary; over the course of Modern English's development, it has borrowed words from over 50 different languages, and many new words have been created from Latin and Greek roots to describe things like scientific discoveries.

Words with Different Meanings

brake—thicket of bushes or trees	list—limit, boundary
cousin—any relative or close friend	marry—an exclamation conveying surprise or contempt
halter—noose	minister—a servant
heavy—sad, oppressive	office—duty or favor
humorous—damp	

All differences aside, Shakespeare's writing had a great influence on the formation of the English language. There are many words that would not exist had it not been for Shakespeare. He actually invented many words of his own. Of course, that practice is frowned upon now. Imagine how your teacher would react if you turned in a paper full of made-up words that only *you* knew the meaning of! But remember that in Shakespeare's time, there were no dictionaries, and the language was so new that there were not the same grammatical rules and conventions that we have today. Therefore, there were very few "right" or "wrong" ways to use a word or a phrase, because no one had yet attempted to write down what was right and what was wrong in terms of grammar. Below is a list of some of Shakespeare's made-up words and phrases.

Words and Phrases Shakespeare Invented	
bedroom	the be-all and the end-all
compromise	It was Greek to me.
dwindle	fair play
negotiate	Knock knock, who's there?
mimic	We have seen better days.
luggage	too much of a good thing
investment	dog will have its day
hurry	vanished into thin air
skim milk	

READING THE BARD

Now that you know the importance of *doing* Shakespeare instead of just sitting back and reading it, you will still find that there are times when you do just have to sit down and read Shakespeare. You will have teachers who will assign you Shakespeare to read, and you will need to come to class with an understanding of what you have read, prepared to answer questions or participate in a discussion.

When this happens, just remember that reading a Shakespeare play does not necessarily mean that you have to retreat to some library by yourself, wading tediously through incomprehensible lines of verse while your mind wanders to more familiar subjects such as what you might like to have for lunch or what movie you will see with your friends this weekend. Of course, if you can concentrate on and understand Shakespeare's plays in such a setting, more power to you! But there are plenty of ways to make reading Shakespeare's plays more fun.

Reading Aloud

As you already know, Shakespeare wrote his plays to be heard, so why not read them out loud? Of course, this option might not go over well in the library, so you will want to find a different spot in which to do it, but you will find reading aloud very rewarding. For one thing, you'll get to hear the beauty and rhythm of the language, and for another, reading it out loud forces you to pay attention to the meaning of the words on the page.

As you read aloud, remember that it does not have to sound perfect, and you do not have to understand absolutely every syllable that comes out of your mouth. You will find, though, that the more you read, the more you will be able to catch the gist of the lines as you say them.

Unless you are using different voices for characters (see below), there is no need to try to sound lofty or British or anything else. You should certainly strive to read with expression, mostly because it will keep you from getting bored by your own monotone, but you can use your normal, everyday voice—the voice you would use to read from the newspaper or your favorite novel.

Do Voices

If you are reading by yourself and are worried about keeping the characters and plot straight in your mind, you might want to try doing different voices for the various characters. You can vary the speed, pitch, volume, and even the dialect or accent for each character. Not only can this help you keep the characters clear in your mind, but it can be very entertaining!

Small Group ACTivity

Choose a scene from a Shakespeare play that involves several different characters. Using a tape recorder, pretend you are making a book on tape—or even doing the voices for a new Shakespeare-based Disney animated film—and tape yourself reading the scene using a suitable voice for each character. Try to make the differentiation in characters very clear. Then, play the tape for your family and friends. Can they tell the difference between the characters? Do the different voices make it easy for them to follow the plot, or is it a distraction?

Definitions

No one expects you to understand every single word the moment you see it. As we discussed earlier, there are a lot of words in Shakespeare that we simply do not use anymore. Whether you want to look up these difficult words as you go or skip over them and save them for later is entirely up to you.

I have had teachers and directors who have been strong advocates for both options. Some have said to me that it is important to understand exactly what I am reading as I read it, and so it is important that I stop to look up any unfamiliar words the moment I come across them. Others have claimed that stopping to look up words will interrupt my train of thought, and that it is more important to get the overall impression of the dialog by trying to read it all at once and worrying about the confusing words later.

I generally compromise. When I read a Shakespeare play, I choose an edition that explains word meanings on the facing page. In other words, the actual text of the play is on every right-hand page, and word definitions, explanations, and scene summaries are on every left-hand page. That way, when I come across a word I do not understand, I can just glance over to the facing page and find out what it means.

Of course, the notes in Shakespeare's plays, including the word definitions, were not written by Shakespeare. They were added later by editors and publishers to make it easier for contemporary readers to understand the play. As a result, different play editions will have different notes. If you have a choice, you should choose the edition with notes that are the easiest for you to understand. Among the editions that are especially good for this type of reading are the *Cambridge School* (Cambridge University Press) editions and the *New Folger Library* (Washington Square Press Drama) editions.

You should decide for yourself how you want to handle the words you do not know. You may choose to look them up immediately in a separate resource, such as C. T. Onions' *A Shakespeare Glossary* (Oxford University Press) or Alexander Schmidt's *Shakespeare Lexicon and Quotation Dictionary* (Dover Publications), both of which can probably be found at your local library. You may choose to mark such words lightly in pencil (if the book belongs to you) or jot them down on a list (if the book belongs to your school or library) and come back to them later. You may choose to skip over them entirely; after all, you may be able to get the gist of what the character is saying by using the context. Or, you could compromise as I do and use an edition with word definitions built in. The only drawback to this is that sometimes there may be words you do not understand that are not defined on the facing page.

Break It Up and Write a Summary

Another thing to remember about reading Shakespeare is that you do not have to read the whole play at once. It can be exhausting to read an entire Shakespeare play in one sitting, especially if you have never done so before.

If you do decide to break up your reading, you should try to write a two- or three-sentence summary of what you have read after each sitting. This will be helpful in two ways: First, when you come back to it, you can refresh your memory as to what just happened when you left off. Second, once you have read and summarized the entire play, your notes will prove to be valuable study aids for an upcoming quiz or class discussion.

Get Some Help

If you have some willing family or friends around, try to get some extra copies of the play from your local or school library, and ask them to read the play aloud with you. In effect, you will have asked them to do a play reading with you. Don't worry about having exactly as many people as there are characters; you can do a play reading with any number of people and just have some people read more than one character. Conversely, if you have more people than characters, you can have two people trade off reading one character's lines. You can assign parts or let them pick their own; if anyone does not like theirs, you can trade halfway through the reading. If you really want to mix things up, don't even assign characters; just have each person read one sentence at a time. That way, no one can zone out while another character has a long *soliloquy*.

> **Soliloquy**
>
> A set of lines spoken by a character who is alone onstage, as if talking to himself or the audience.

Read It Again

Whatever reading method you choose, you should explore the benefits of reading the play more than once. After all, when you go to see a Shakespeare play, the actors are able to make it look so effortless because they have read the script hundreds of times. Each time you read a play, you will grow a little more familiar with the plot and characters, but you will also keep discovering new things. Even if you choose to break the play up into manageable pieces, such as reading it one act at a time, you can read each act over and over until you are comfortable that you have understood it and could discuss it thoroughly.

Using Published Summaries

The last suggestion I can offer to help you in reading Shakespeare is made with a great degree of caution: play summaries. There are a lot of great ones out there, from children's illustrated storybooks to the well-known *Cliff's Notes*. There are even some editions of the actual plays that contain summaries as well. The aforementioned *Cambridge School* and *Folger Shakespeare Library* editions, for instance, use summaries at the beginning of each scene.

But *never*, under any circumstances, read a play summary without reading the actual play! Even the man who invented *Cliff's Notes*, Cliff Hillegass, said that he never intended for *Cliff's Notes* to be used by themselves, but rather in conjunction with the original texts. Play summaries are simply a tool for appreciating great literature, not a replacement for it. If you use only the play summaries, you will miss Shakespeare's beautiful language and subtle mode of expression. You will miss the jokes and the interplay between characters. You will miss what makes Shakespeare uniquely Shakespeare.

Take, for instance, Act III, Scene i of *Hamlet*. The beginning of the scene finds the King and Queen questioning Hamlet's buddies, Rosencrantz and Guildenstern. Hamlet's friends express real concern for him, and honest confusion about his strange behavior—and this makes it all the more obvious that Hamlet's stepfather, Claudius, doesn't care about him at all. But in the *Cliff's Notes* summary of this scene, Rosencrantz and Guildenstern are not even mentioned. Later on in the scene is Hamlet's famous "To be or not to be" speech. It is a fascinating glimpse of Hamlet's despair and confusion—he is so upset that he is considering committing suicide, but is worried about what will happen to his soul if he does. The language Hamlet uses to contemplate suicide has become famous. And yet the *Cliff's Notes* summary explains the whole 34-line monologue with one sentence: "Hamlet muses about life and death in his fourth and most famous soliloquy" (Lamb 101). Doesn't that seem a little too simple? It is only by delving into the original text that you could truly discover Rosencrantz and Guildenstern's honest attempt to cheer up their friend Hamlet, and Hamlet's teetering on the edge of self-destruction.

Reading a scene or act and then reading the summary of it can help to cement the plot and characters in your mind. But don't read the summary before you read the play. Have confidence in your own ability to get through Shakespeare's language without having to lean on simplified play summaries.

Solo ACTivity

Choose two scenes from two different plays. Read one scene out loud once; read the other silently to yourself once. Then, try to write a detailed summary of each scene. Which scene is easier to remember? Why?

KEEPING TRACK OF CHARACTERS

As you read a Shakespeare play, you may have difficulty keeping track of the characters. Sometimes character names are similar to each other; sometimes it's just that their names are so unusual, at least by 21st century American standards, that you can't remember who is who. And, of course, all of Shakespeare's plays simply have a *lot* of characters, and you will need a way to tell them apart as you read.

Dramatis Personae

At the beginning of each play, you will see a list called **Dramatis Personae**. This is Latin for "people in the play." It is simply a list of all of the characters who appear in the play. If it

DRAMATIS PERSONAE
A list of characters in a play.

helps, you can make a copy of this list and keep it handy as you read, so that you have it to refer to whenever a new character comes in.

Sometimes several characters will have the same first name. This is especially prevalent in the history plays, because English kings often gave their own names to their eldest sons. It was also fashionable for noblemen to name their sons after a beloved king. This resulted in a lot of Henrys, Richards, and Edwards. When a character's line comes up in the text, the editor may use the character's title or nickname to make it clear which Henry or Richard is speaking. Once you figure out what name is used to designate which character, try writing it beside the character's name in your photocopy of the Dramatis Personae. That way, when someone called "Bolingbroke" speaks in *Richard II*, you will know it is the character referred to in the Dramatis Personae as "Henry Bolingbroke, Duke of Hereford, son to John of Gaunt, and later King Henry IV," and not Sir Henry Green or Henry Percy, Earl of Northumberland.

The Dramatis Personae is generally divided into two sections: the male characters first, and then the female characters. Each of those two sections is broken down so that the major characters are listed first, in order of social status. So you will see kings and princes first, then dukes and barons, merchants, farmers, and servants. (Character lists in modern-day plays usually put the characters in order of how big their roles are; in other words, the character with the most lines is at the top of the list, with the character with the least lines at the bottom.) You can see that the Elizabethans' belief in the "Great Chain of Being" described in chapter one extended even to lists of characters in plays.

After some of the character names, you will see a phrase such as "brother to Ophelia" or "servant of the king." This phrase is crucial in determining the characters' relationship to one another. Once you determine the characters' relationships, it is easier to understand how and why they interact as they do.

Especially in Shakespeare's comedies, you will find that some of the characters have no relationship to one another because they are in different story lines. This is called **subplot**. A subplot is a separate story woven into the main story, and, in some cases, reflecting the events of the main plot. It is sort of like a modern-day television soap opera in that there are several different story lines and you see small snippets of each one as they unfold; that is, the action switches frequently among the different stories. In Shakespeare's comedies, especially, all the different stories end up getting tied together at the end, often as pairs of characters from different plots get married at the same time.

SUBPLOT

A secondary plot in a play or story.

Family Tree

It is important to tie together as many of the characters as you can, so as to keep track of them. There are a couple of effective ways to do this. The first is making a family tree. Of course, not all characters in a play are actually related—at least, not by blood—so you will have to find other ways of indicating relationships. Some family trees look like actual trees; others simply look like charts, with lines connecting various people to one another. You can draw a variation of a family tree for any Shakespeare play; you will simply have to come up with your own way of denoting each type of relationship. For instance, you could use different colors or different types of lines to show all the usual family relations, plus others such as "in love with," "enemy of," "neighbor of," and "servant to." You may not be able to glean all of this information from the Dramatis Personae, which is why you should leave space to add to or alter your family tree as you read and discover more about the ways in which the characters are interconnected.

Visual Cues

Another option for keeping all the characters straight in your head is to use visual cues. Choose anything that means something to you—assign each character a different color, draw a portrait of the way you think each character would look, or use magazine cutouts of celebrity faces to go with each character. That way, you have a concrete visual cue to associate with the character's name, so that whenever that name appears in the script, you will not be continually saying, "Who's that?"

Tell me again, how do I read Shakespeare?

Here is a list that summarizes the tips above for reading Shakespeare's plays and keeping track of the characters as you read. You can use as many of them as you want, and in any combination.

- Read it out loud
- Do a different voice for each character
- Look up definitions for unknown words
- Break it up into manageable pieces
- Write summaries of what you have read
- Get family and friends to read with you
- Read it more than once
- Use play summaries (with original text!)
- Copy the Dramatis Personae
- Make a family tree of the characters
- Assign a picture or color to each character

Solo ACTivity

Choose a Shakespearean play and, using the Dramatis Personae, make a chart of all the characters. You can draw a picture of each character, use colors to tell them apart, or use abstract symbols to denote each character. Make sure your chart also shows the relationship between the characters. Then, read the play (or one act or scene of it) and see whether your chart helped your understanding of the play. If you need to, go back to your chart and make any required changes or additions as you read the play, based on what you've learned about the characters.

PROSE VERSUS VERSE

In Shakespeare's time, people sometimes used the word "poet" when referring to a playwright. You may have heard Shakespeare referred to as a poet and wondered, "Wait, I thought he wrote plays!" Actually, Shakespeare wrote some beautiful poetry outside of his plays. He also used poetry *in* his plays: This is more commonly called "verse."

Verse should be familiar to you because it is used in music. If you think of your favorite song, you will notice that the words not only rhyme, but fit into a specific rhythm. But words do not have to be set to music in order to be called verse. Saying that something is written in verse just means that each line has a certain number of syllables and therefore fits into a certain rhythm, and that the words at the ends of the lines sometimes rhyme. Verse that rhymes is called, obviously enough, "rhyming verse," while verse that does not rhyme is called *blank verse*.

BLANK VERSE

Iambic pentameter verse that does not rhyme.

Prose, on the other hand, is what you are reading right now. Newspaper and magazine articles, novels, most contemporary plays, and textbooks, just to name a few, are written in prose. Prose is the ordinary language people use when speaking.

PROSE

Ordinary language in which people write and speak, as opposed to poetic verse.

Before Shakespeare's time, most plays were written in verse. Sometimes the verse rhymed, sometimes it did not, but it usually followed conventions such as how many syllables were in each line.

Just because Shakespeare and all the playwrights who preceded him wrote in verse does not mean people of the time spoke in verse. It was simply considered the proper way to write. It was formal and dignified, and, on a more practical level, it was easier to memorize. Think about it: What would be easier for you to remember, the preamble to the U.S. Constitution, or the words to your favorite song? If something has a rhythm and it rhymes, it is easier to learn quickly than something that has a varied meter and no rhymes at all.

Shakespeare was the first to mix prose and verse in his plays. He always did it very carefully, and for good reasons. Sometimes he would have characters who were poor or stupid speak in prose, to set them apart from the characters in the play who were rich, educated, and high-born, and who spoke in verse. This is yet another manifestation of the Elizabethan tendency to rank people according to their birth: It was perfectly natural to think that someone who was born into a working-class family would not be able to speak in verse, while someone born to nobility would speak in fluid poetry.

An excellent example of this is in *A Midsummer Night's Dream*. This play has several of the aforementioned subplots that weave together at the end. One of the subplots concerns a group of tradesmen who want to put on a play in honor of the Duke of Athens' wedding. The tradesmen, who are bumbling, silly, and not terribly smart or well-educated, always speak in prose. All the other characters in the play speak in verse. This is true even when one of the tradesmen is speaking with another character. For instance, in Act III, Scene i, Titania, Queen of the Fairies, meets and falls in love with the tradesman Bottom, a weaver. While Bottom bumbles along in prose, Titania declares her love for him in lovely, rhyming verse:

> BOTTOM: *Not so neither; but if I had wit enough to get out of this wood,*
> *I have enough to serve mine own turn.*
>
> TITANIA: *Out of this wood do not desire to go.*
> *Thou shalt remain here whether thou wilt or no.*
> *I am a spirit of no common rate.*
> *The summer still doth tend upon my state,*
> *And I do love thee. Therefore go with me.*

Occasionally, a character who would ordinarily speak in verse speaks in prose. This is Shakespeare's way of showing that the character is too tired, insane, or otherwise distracted to speak in verse. For instance, in *King Lear*, we see the King slipping in and out of madness as he switches from speaking verse to prose to verse again. In *Hamlet*, the changes are more calculated. Hamlet speaks prose in more casual circumstances with his friends, and speaks in verse when he is at court with his mother and stepfather. The exception is when he wants to make his parents think he is crazy or otherwise confuse them, in which case he speaks prose while they speak verse. In this case, verse is clearly delineated as the proper language of the court, while prose is for less formal occasions. It is for this reason that Hamlet chooses to provoke anger in his elders by using the "improper" prose; he knows the right buttons to push!

When you are reading a passage in verse, it may help you to understand a little bit more about the structure of the verse itself. Once you start acting Shakespeare, an understanding of the verse is even more important because it will help you to get the meaning across to your audience.

SCANSION

SCANSION

The analysis of poetic verse.

Anyone can read Shakespeare out loud. It takes a little more work to read Shakespeare so that others can understand what is being read. This process is called *scansion*. It is the study of metrical verse.

PROLOGUE

An introduction or preface to a play, poem, book, etc.

To help illustrate each new concept in scansion, we will use as an example the ***prologue*** from *Romeo and Juliet*. This particular passage is very popular for teaching scansion, for several reasons: It contains all of the elements of Shakespearean rhyming verse in one neat, 14-line package; it is at the beginning of a play and therefore does not require the reader to know any preceding plot points; since it is a prologue, it is self-contained; and since it is from a play rather than a sonnet, it is easier to identify the character speaking.

Two households, both alike in dignity

In fair Verona where we lay our scene,

From ancient grudge break to new mutiny,

Where civil blood makes civil hands unclean.

From forth the fatal loins of these two foes

A pair of star-crossed lovers take their life;

Whose misadventured piteous overthrows

Doth with their death bury their parents' strife.

The fearful passage of their death-marked love

And the continuance of their parents' rage,

Which, but their children's end, naught could remove,

Is now the two hours' traffic of our stage.

The which, if you with patient ears attend,

What here shall miss, our toil shall strive to mend.

Most of the time, when Shakespeare wrote in verse, he used a form of verse called **iambic pentameter**. Iambic pentameter is, as the last part of the phrase would suggest, a "meter," very much like the meter in music. Most music has a time signature—often 4/4 time, or four quarter notes to each measure—which results in a specific beat that you can tap your toe or snap your fingers to. Shakespeare's verse also has a specific beat, and when that beat is iambic pentameter, it means that there are five iambs (or "feet") per line. The prefix "penta" means five, as in a five-sided pentagon. An "iamb," or foot, is a little more obscure. It is a set of two syllables, the first of which is unstressed, and the second of which is stressed, so it sounds like this: dah-DUM. The word "repair" is an iamb: re-PAIR. An iamb does not have to be one word, however; the phrase "to be" is also an iamb: to BE.

> **IAMBIC PENTAMETER**
>
> A rhythm used in verse. Each line in iambic pentameter has five iambs. An iamb is a pair of syllables, the first unstressed, the second stressed.

So, in a perfect line of iambic pentameter, there should be ten syllables, every other one of which is stressed. As an example, let's look at the first line of the prologue from *Romeo and Juliet:* "Two households, both alike in dignity." If you exaggerate the sound of the iambic pentameter, it sounds like this: "Two HOUSE-holds BOTH a-LIKE in DIG-ni-TY." Notice that there are five syllables in bold: five iambs, or iambic pentameter.

Learning to stress every other syllable is just the tip of the iceberg, though. After all, if you read a whole Shakespeare play out loud in a strict "dah-DUM dah-DUM dah-DUM dah-DUM dah-DUM" singsong, you would fall asleep from boredom just as surely as if you were reading the play silently to yourself! It is not the meter that makes Shakespeare's poetry so beautiful; rather, it is how he works within such a strict structure—and eventually breaks the rules. Following are a few more guidelines to keep in mind as you read his verse aloud.

Understanding the Words

We have already talked about finding word definitions as you are reading a Shakespeare text for the first or second time. As you prepare a text to be recited in class or even acted on stage, a specific understanding of every single word is absolutely necessary. A general understanding of the basic meaning of the play is fine for reading the script through once or twice, but your understanding must be much more detailed for performance. If you do not understand the words that are coming out of your mouth, you cannot possibly expect your audience to understand them.

If you are preparing a speech or perhaps a scene with another character, write out your own translation, or paraphrase, of it line by line. Start by marking the words in the speech that you do not understand. Remember that some of the words that look familiar to you may have had different meanings in Shakespeare's time. If a word you already know is in a strange context—that is, if it is used in a way you would not ordinarily use it—that may be your clue that you will need to look it up.

Once you have a list of unknown words, look them up and choose what you consider to be the best definition—the one that makes the most sense in the context of the speech. You can either look up unknown words in Onions or Schmidt (both glossaries were mentioned earlier in this chapter), or you can go to the mother of all dictionaries, the *Oxford English Dictionary*. Your library may have a copy of the whole multi-volume set, and there is also a CD-ROM version available. The great thing about the *OED* (as it is called for short) is that it lists every meaning a word ever had, and also lists the first documented time the word was ever used.

Once you have looked up and chosen the meanings of the word, fit them into your line-by-line translation. As an example, let's look at the first few lines of the prologue:

> *Two households, both alike in dignity*
> *In fair Verona, where we lay our scene,*
> *From ancient grudge break to new mutiny,*
> *Where civil blood makes civil hands unclean.*

The words we need to look up are *household, dignity, fair, ancient, break, mutiny*, and *civil*. Here are definitions for each:

> *household:* family
> *dignity:* worthiness or merit
> *fair:* beautiful
> *ancient:* long-standing
> *break:* to open
> *mutiny:* discord
> *civil:* relating to the community

Using these definitions, here is a paraphrase of the first four lines of the prologue. Note that the translation itself does not have to be in iambic pentameter, since you will not be speaking your translation aloud. It is just a tool for you to use.

> Two families of equal worthiness
> In beautiful Verona, where our play is set,
> From a long-standing grudge, open up a new argument
> That spills the blood of some community members,
> making other community members' hands dirty.

Once you have paraphrased the passage and are sure you understand it, it is time to go back to the real words, so that you can get the meaning across to your audience.

Small Group ACTivity

Choose a passage from Shakespeare with which you are not familiar. Read it aloud twice to an audience: first, before you have paraphrased it, and again after. (Remember, you are paraphrasing just for your own understanding. Read the actual text to them the second time, not the paraphrase). Both times, have the audience write a summary of what the passage is about. Then, compare their summaries and discuss. Did your audience understand the passage better when **you** understood it better?

Exceptions to the Rule

Now that you understand the rhythm of iambic pentameter, it is time to learn about the exceptions. After all, it would probably be impossible to fit everything into ten neat little syllables per line, but when the words do not quite fit into the meter, it just makes it sound more interesting.

For instance, sometimes there are more than ten syllables in a line. In this case, you have a couple of options: give every syllable its full value and pause at the end of the line, or condense a word to make it fit. The more you do this, the easier it will be to tell which solution is appropriate.

Going back to the *Romeo and Juliet* prologue, you will see that line 7 has too many syllables: "Whose misadventured piteous overthrows," or, stressing the iambs, "whose MIS-ad-VEN-tured PI-te-OUS O-ver-THROWS." You will notice that there are six stressed syllables, rather than five, plus there are two stressed syllables next to each other without an unstressed one in between. How to fix this? Make the word "piteous" two syllables instead of three; in other words, condense it: "PI-tyus." Now try line 7 again: "Whose MIS-ad-VEN-tured PI-teous O-ver-THROWS." And there you have it: ten syllables, five stressed, five unstressed.

To find an example of a line with more than ten syllables that cannot be fixed by condensing the words, we have to go beyond the *Romeo and Juliet* prologue. Hamlet's famous "To be or not to be" speech (Act III, Scene i) is full of lines like this. When a line ends in an eleventh, unstressed syllable, it is called a "weak" ending. But when a line has the usual ten syllables and therefore ends in a strong, stressed syllable, it is called a "strong" ending. The first four lines of Hamlet's speech have weak endings:

> *To BE or NOT to BE—that IS the QUES-tion:*
> *Whe-THER 'tis NOB-ler IN the MIND to SUF-fer*
> *The SLINGS and AR-rows OF out-RA-geous FOR-tune*
> *Or TO take ARMS a-GAINST a SEA of TROU-bles*

Try saying the lines out loud. You will find that, in order to make it sound right and not trip up on your words, you have to take the tiniest pause between two unstressed syllables—in this case, between the end of one line and the beginning of the next. When lines have strong endings, they flow effortlessly into one another. However, a weak ending—especially several in one speech—gives the impression that the speaker is upset or angry. In this case, Hamlet is angry at his mother and stepfather, upset about the death of his father, and contemplating suicide. How could someone in such a state fit their thoughts into ten neat syllables per line? The weak endings are Shakespeare's way of showing us the turmoil that Hamlet is going through.

Punctuation

It is important to note that, just because a text is divided into lines, you do not have to read it that way. In fact, the only time you should pause at the end of a line is in the case of a weak ending (a tiny pause) or some sort of punctuation (a bigger pause). Punctuation can be the key to meaning. It can tell you when to pause, which phrases are separate and which are together, when to shout, and when to raise your voice in a question. Just remember that, over the years, some editors have changed the punctuation. For this reason it may be useful to compare two or three versions of the text, and use the punctuation that makes the most sense to you.

Solo ACTivity

What would Shakespeare sound like if he wrote today? Translate a scene of your choice from a Shakespearean play. Use the language you use every day to put the scene into your own words while fully retaining the meaning. Feel free to use slang, but not profanity. **Scene Suggestions:** *Romeo and Juliet*, Act I, Scene i; *As You Like It*, Act I, Scene iii; *Hamlet*, Act III, Scene i.

Repeated Sounds and Words

Finding the repeated sounds and words in a Shakespeare text will help you figure out which words are important, and will also bring out the beauty of the poetry. There are four categories of these: rhyme, assonance, alliteration, and repeated words.

Rhyme

Of course, you know what a *rhyme* is. If two words rhyme, their final syllable shares the same vowel sound, accent, and final consonant sound (for example: believe/retrieve, bear/hair, right/polite). Rhymes are sounds that the modern human ear is still attuned to, so there is usually no need to stress rhyming words—they tend to emphasize themselves.

> **RHYME**
>
> Words with the same ending sound, most often in the ends of lines of verse.

There are two types of rhymes. The most obvious rhymes are end-of-line rhymes; for instance, the ends of every other line in the prologue rhyme, as do the last two. When two consecutive lines of iambic pentameter rhyme, this is called a "rhyming couplet." If you look and listen carefully, you will find that Shakespeare uses rhyming couplets very frequently, most often to signal the end of a scene or act. It is sort of like a verbal curtain closing on the scene. Here are the last two lines of the prologue:

> *The which, if you with patient ears at-TEND,*
> *What here shall miss, our toil shall strive to MEND.*

The other type of rhyme is easier to miss. It is called an internal rhyme, and it happens when there are rhyming words within a line, rather than at the end. There is an internal rhyme in the second line of the prologue:

> *In FAIR Verona, WHERE we lay our scene,*

You will notice that, so far, the words that rhyme are also the stressed syllables in iambic pentameter. This is a clue that these words deserve a little more weight than the others.

Assonance

Assonance is the repetition of vowel sounds. This occurs much more than internal rhymes, and it is fun to play with when reading the text out loud. Assonance is not necessarily obvious right away, but if you know to look for it, it can show you what words should stand out. For an excellent example of assonance, let's look at the first two lines of *Richard III*:

> **ASSONANCE**
>
> The repetition of vowel sounds in two or more words in a phrase. The phrase from *Romeo and Juliet*, "My name, dear saint, is hateful to myself" (Act II, Scene ii) repeats a long "a" sound using the words "name," "saint," and "hateful."

> *Now IS the WIN-ter of our DIS-content*
> *Made GLOR-ious summer by this son of YORK*

You will notice that in the first line, the repeated vowel sound is an "ih," whereas in the second line, it is an "or" sound. Again, we see that the repeated sounds fall on the stressed syllables of the line—and when you speak these lines out loud, you will certainly sound discontented!

Alliteration

This is one you might already be familiar with. **Alliteration** is the repetition of consonants. They usually stand out more when they are at the beginnings of words, but they can be anywhere. Line 5 of the *Romeo and Juliet* prologue uses some great alliteration with F's:

> **ALLITERATION**
>
> The repetition of the first letter or sound of two or more words in a phrase, The phrase "A fond farewell" uses alliteration with the "F" sound.

> *From Forth the Fatal loins of these two Foes*

When you say this line and use the repeated "F" sounds for emphasis, it gives the line more meaning and even makes the meaning clearer.

Repeated Words

These are probably the least frequent of all the repeated sounds in Shakespeare. Conveniently, however, there happens to be an instance of repeated words in the *Romeo and Juliet* prologue:

> *Where CIVIL blood makes CIVIL hands unclean.*

With repeated words, you have two choices. You can either stress the repeated words themselves, or you can stress the word after, to set off the difference between the two phrases:

> *Where civil BLOOD makes civil HANDS unclean.*

In this particular case, it may be better to stress the words "blood" and "hands," as they are also stressed syllables according to iambic pentameter.

When in Doubt: Nouns and Verbs

If you are ever in a quandary as to what words to stress in a line—if, for instance, there are no repeated sounds and the punctuation does not help—you cannot go wrong with stressing the nouns and verbs. After all, those are the most important words when we are trying to get a point across. Adverbs, adjectives, and prepositions are nice, but when you really need to know what is going on, look to the nouns and verbs. A noun-and-verb reading of the first four lines of the prologue would look like this:

> *Two HOUSEHOLDS, BOTH alike in DIGNITY*
> *In fair VERONA, where WE LAY our SCENE,*
> *From ancient GRUDGE BREAK to new MUTINY,*
> *Where civil BLOOD MAKES civil HANDS unclean.*

Even if you did not know anything more about the play, you would know by looking at the nouns and verbs in this passage that you are watching a scene set in Verona about two evenly matched households with a grudge who start a new fight, and blood gets on someone's hands. That pretty much sums up the way *Romeo and Juliet* starts off, doesn't it?

Stressed Out?

With so much talk of when to stress what, you may be saying to yourself, "If I follow all these rules, every single word will be stressed!" When you get to feeling this way, remember two important things:

1. Knowing what the text actually means will help you know what is most important to stress.
2. In the end, it is up to you. There is no "perfect" way to mark up text.

With these things in mind, then, you can devise your own system of marking up a text. Marking up a text is a way of making notations so that, when you read it out loud, you know what words to stress, and which stressed ones should have more weight. You can use accent marks ($\checkmark$), underlines, circled words, or even use different colors of highlighter pen (although I would recommend only doing this on a photocopy, and not in a real book)— whatever catches your eye and helps you to remember how you want to get the meaning across.

A Quick Reference Guide to Scansion

1. Read through the passage, making a list of the words you do not understand.
2. Look up the words in a Shakespeare glossary.
3. Using the definitions, write a paraphrase of the passage.
4. Mark the iambic pentameter, taking note of weak endings and condensed words.
5. Examine the punctuation and decide how to use it.
6. Mark rhymes, both internal and end-of-line.
7. Mark assonances.
8. Mark alliterations.
9. Mark repeated words.
10. Mark the nouns and verbs you want to stand out.
11. Read the passage aloud as you have marked it, compare it to your paraphrase, and make any necessary changes.

A Sample Markup and Paraphrase

I have included an example of my own markup of the prologue from *Romeo and Juliet*. The accent marks indicate the rhythm of iambic pentameter, the circled words are the ones I want to say with the most stress, and the underlined letters are sounds I want to bring out. Following the markup is a paraphrase I referred to while making my markup, in case I forgot the meaning of the line and needed to remember what words should get the most emphasis.

Sample Markup

Two households, both alike in dignity
In fair Verona where we lay our scene,
From ancient grudge break to new mutiny,
Where civil blood makes civil hands unclean.
From forth the fatal loins of these two foes
A pair of star-crossed lovers take their life;
Whose misadventured piteous overthrows
Doth with their death bury their parents' strife.
The fearful passage of their death-marked love
And the continuance of their parents' rage,
Which, but their children's end, naught could remove,
Is now the two hours' traffic of our stage.
The which, if you with patient ears attend,
What here shall miss, our toil shall strive to mend.

Sample Paraphrase

Two families of equal worthiness

In beautiful Verona, where our play is set,

From a long-standing grudge, open up a new argument

That spills the blood of some community members, making other community members' hands dirty.

Out of the doomed bloodlines of these two enemies

A pair of unfortunate children are born and fall in love;

Whose unfortunate miserable ruin

Bury their parents' arguments by dying.

The terrible course of their doomed love

And permanence of their parents' hate for one another,

Which nothing could stop except their children's death,

Are the events that will be on our stage for the next two hours;

Which, if you will listen indulgently,

We will work to fill you in if you missed anything I just said.

Small Group ACTivity

Go through all the steps of scansion for a short verse passage of your choice. Discuss which words are more important to stress, and why. Make a markup of the passage. If necessary, compare readings out loud to decide which is better.

Section Two

STUDYING SHAKESPEARE:
PLAYS AND CHARACTERS

THE FOUR TYPES OF PLAYS

"The best actors in the world, either for tragedy, comedy, history, pastoral, pastoral-comical, historical-pastoral, tragical-historical, tragical-comical-historical-pastoral, scene individable, or poem unlimited."

—*Hamlet*, ACT II, SCENE II, LINES 420–424

COMMON THREADS
AMONG SHAKESPEARE'S PLAYS

A common joke among Shakespeare enthusiasts is that you know it's a comedy when everyone gets married at the end, but it's a tragedy when everyone is dead at the end. Of course, this isn't true in all cases, and even if it were, it wouldn't be the only major difference between Shakespeare's comedies and tragedies. And he did write more than just those two types of plays. But for the most part, there is some truth in the joke. There isn't a lot of death in Shakespeare's comedies (and when there is, the dead person often miraculously comes back to life), and there aren't a lot of weddings in Shakespeare's tragedies (and when there are, the marriage often turns sour and ends in—you guessed it—someone's death).

All of Shakespeare's plays—whether comedies, tragedies, histories, or romances—have certain aspects in common. We'll look first at these common threads before we begin to study each individual type of play.

Structure

One of the most obvious (and therefore, most misleading) things that all of Shakespeare's plays have in common is their structure. Every Shakespeare play has five acts—that is, they're all divided into five major sections.

However, most experts agree that the plays were divided into acts long after Shakespeare wrote them. In other words, each of his plays was originally just one long, continuous set of dialogue, and years later editors came along and divided it into acts and scenes to make it easier to stage and read. Most of the divisions occurred at places where there is a change of location, or where one group of characters leaves the stage and another group enters. But the point is that Shakespeare was not bound by some pre-determined five-act structure in writing his plays. He did not follow any outline that suggested that, for instance, the main character had to meet his future wife in Act III and marry her in Act V.

Exposition

In the first act of a Shakespeare play, there is often some exposition. By discussing events that have happened in the past, characters reveal what you need to know to understand the background of the story. (It's kind of like the giant scrolling words at the beginning of *Star Wars* that tell you what has happened up to this point, only it is cleverly worked into a scene between characters so you don't realize you're watching exposition.)

EXPOSITION

An explanation of what has happened in the characters' lives up to the point when the play starts.

For example, in order to fully understand what happens in *Hamlet*, there are a few things we need to know about what's been going on in Denmark. Shakespeare has several interesting ways of incorporating this exposition into Act I. In Act I, Scene i, when the soldiers on the battlements of the castle first see the ghost of Hamlet's father, they ask Horatio to explain what it might mean. Horatio thinks it might be an omen of war, and as he explains why, he reveals valuable information that will help us understand the rest of the play:

> *Our last king,*
> *Whose image even now appeared to us,*
> *Was, as you know, by Fortinbras of Norway*

...Dar'd to the combat; in which our valiant Hamlet

...Did slay this Fortinbras; who, by a seal'd compact,

...Did forfeit with his life all those his lands

Which he stood seiz'd of, to the conqueror.

...Now, sir, young Fortinbras,

of unimproved mettle hot and full,

...But to recover of us, by strong hand

and terms compulsative, those foresaid lands

so by his father lost. And this, I take it,

Is the main motive of our preparations,

the source of this our watch...

(Selected lines from Act I, Scene i, Lines 80–106)

It seems that Hamlet's father, the King of Denmark at the time, had declared war against King Fortinbras of Norway. He'd killed Fortinbras and had taken a lot of his land. Fortinbras' son, whose name is also Fortinbras, is angry, and Denmark is preparing for another war should the younger Fortinbras decide to try to win back his father's lands. It is crucial for us to know this information, even though it took place before the action of the play starts, because the younger Fortinbras figures prominently in the tragic end of the play.

Later on in Act I, Shakespeare continues the exposition in the form of a speech Claudius makes to his family and advisors. Here, he explains that his brother the king has recently died, and that Claudius himself has taken over both his crown and his wife, and is now Hamlet's stepfather:

Though yet of Hamlet our dear brother's death

The memory be green...

Therefore our sometime sister, now our queen,

Th'imperial jointress to this war-like state,

Have we...Taken to wife.

(Selected lines from Act I, Scene ii, Lines 1–14)

This sets the stage for Hamlet's unhappiness, and therefore for much of the rest of the action in the play.

Conflict

Like *Hamlet*, all of Shakespeare's plays use exposition to explain what you need to know about the story. Once you're brought up to speed, it's time to introduce **conflict**. It's pretty safe to say that all plays—not just Shakespeare's—revolve around conflict of some sort. And by the end of Shakespeare's plays, the conflict is always resolved. Tragedies usually have a sad **resolution** to the conflict, such as death, whereas the conflict resolution at the end of comedies tends to be happy.

CONFLICT

The opposition of two characters or groups that cause the dramatic action in a play.

RESOLUTION

In a play, the point at which the main problem is worked out.

The nature of the conflict, of course, varies greatly. In *Hamlet* there are many—one of them is that Hamlet is very upset about his father's murder but doesn't know how to carry out his father's wishes. In *As You Like It,* one of the major conflicts is that Rosalind is in love with Orlando, but circumstances require that she hide her true identity from him. Both of these conflicts are resolved at the end of their respective plays. In *Hamlet*, death is the unhappy resolution; in *As You Like It*, Rosalind sets up a surprise wedding for herself and Orlando and reveals her identity to him at the last moment.

Change

Another common characteristic of Shakespeare's plays—one that is a result of conflict—is that the main characters are somehow changed. They are different at the end than they were at the beginning, having learned something, suffered a great loss, made an important decision, or fallen in love, just to name a few examples. In *As You Like It,* Rosalind goes from being the obedient, quiet girl we meet at the beginning of the play to a confident woman in charge of her own destiny. In *Hamlet*, Hamlet finds, with his own life in peril, that he does in fact have the strength and courage to avenge his father's death.

One of the things that makes Shakespeare so unique for his time is that his plays are character-driven. In other words, even though the plots are interesting, what is truly compelling is the way Shakespeare makes his characters react to, and behave inside, the plots. And while the force of his characters is often strong enough to change the plot, what is most interesting is the way the characters themselves have changed as a result of everything they've been through.

In this respect, Shakespeare's plays are very realistic. It's a fact of life that people change. You are a different person from the one you were a year ago because of what you have learned, seen, and experienced. You may be radically different or only slightly different, but you have changed. And the reason we can identify with Shakespeare's characters so easily is that they change, too.

Subplots

Many of Shakespeare's plays also contain subplots. The subplots have most of the same characteristics as the main story: There may be a little exposition involved (although not as much as is needed for the main plot); there is conflict; the conflict is resolved at the end; and the characters are somehow changed.

The great thing about subplots is that, while they may start out being totally unrelated to the main story, they usually get woven in at the end. Because of this, the resolution of the main story usually leads to the resolution of the subplots as well.

For example, in *As You Like It*, there are a couple of different subplots. In one, a shepherd named Silvius is in love with a shepherdess named Phoebe who doesn't love him back, which is of course the conflict. When Rosalind stages her surprise wedding at the end, Silvius and Phoebe get roped into getting married as well, so Rosalind's resolution also leads to the resolution of the subplot. And of course, Phoebe has changed in that she now believes she could grow to love Silvius.

Laughter Through Tears

Later on in this chapter, we will discuss what makes a comedy a comedy and a *tragedy* a tragedy, but before we do that, there is something you should understand. Comedies aren't necessarily constantly funny, and tragedies aren't always sad. In Shakespeare's

TRAGEDY

A genre of plays characterized by the protagonist's unsuccessful struggle against forces beyond his or her control, which usually end in disaster.

61

case, there are often sad parts in comedy and funny parts in tragedy. This is a good thing, because laughing for three hours straight can be exhausting, and witnessing three hours of nothing but sadness could be just as bad. Instead, Shakespeare sometimes gives us a break, and by doing so, makes us appreciate the rest of the play that much more.

In *King Lear*, there is a whole character set aside just for comic relief. The Fool, Lear's court jester, is always around to at least try to cheer up the king. He is always ready with a pun, a joke, or a song, and while he doesn't always make King Lear (or us) laugh, he at least gives us a chance to catch our breath and get some perspective on the situation.

Similarly, the silliness and fun of *Much Ado About Nothing* is put on hold for a scene when the characters are led to believe that Hero is dead. While we as the audience know that she is alive, it is still sad to see her fiancé, Claudio, visit her tomb. The song that is sung at her grave is a sobering reminder that the rollicking fun of life can end suddenly. And it is also a clever plot device, making the ending that much happier when Claudio discovers Hero isn't dead after all. The sadness makes us appreciate the happiness more.

Solo ACTivity

The next time you sit down to watch your favorite sitcom or TV drama, take some notes on the plot and subplot. Does the episode tell only one story, or does it interweave two or more? Does the subplot parallel the main plot? How? If the main plot is funny, is the subplot sad, or vice versa? Are any characters involved in both plots? How are the plot and subplot resolved?

SHAKESPEARE'S COMEDIES

Now that we have learned the basics of Shakespeare's play structure, it is time to examine in more detail the four types of plays. Most scholars agree that the following Shakespeare plays fall into the category of comedy:

The Comedy of Errors
The Taming of the Shrew
The Two Gentlemen of Verona
Love's Labor's Lost
A Midsummer Night's Dream
The Merchant of Venice
The Merry Wives of Windsor
Much Ado About Nothing
As You Like It
Twelfth Night

It is important to understand that the definition of comedy has changed since Shakespeare's time. Today, the word "comedy" often refers to anything that is funny. But comedy in Shakespeare's time usually referred to a play with a happy ending. One of the things that sets Shakespeare's comedies and tragedies apart from one another is their contrasting views of the world. In a comic view, bad things do happen, but we are able to laugh at our mistakes and weaknesses because we know that everything will turn out all right in the end. In a tragic view, we realize that no matter what we do (or even *because* of what we do), things are destined to go badly, and we are mere pawns in fate's plan. So you can see that while Shakespeare's comedies happen to be funny, the jokes and puns are not what make them comedies.

The "Rules" of Comedy

GENRE

A category of artistic composition (such as plays) usually characterized by its form and content. Comedies, tragedies, histories, and romances are all examples of different genres.

FARCE

A style of comedy with a far-fetched or even ridiculous plot and broad, stylized characters.

SATIRE

A type of comedy that makes fun of human mistakes using sarcasm and scorn.

SLAPSTICK

A type of comedy focused on silly, clumsy, physical humor. When we laugh at people falling down or running into doors, we are laughing at slapstick.

The *genre* of comedy existed long before Shakespeare began writing plays. In fact, the ancient Greeks actually had rules as to what a comedy should be:

1. The ancient Greeks insisted that comedies deal strictly with the "low-born." They didn't think it was appropriate for audiences to be laughing at princes or kings.

2. Comedies generally dealt with the here and now; most of the subject matter was about current affairs, as opposed to great battles or other historical moments.

3. Comedies often involved several types of humor, including *farce*, *satire*, and *slapstick* humor.

Shakespeare was born about 2,000 years after these rules were made. Although the rules were still being used during Shakespeare's lifetime, he didn't seem particularly concerned with abiding by them. For instance, Shakespeare was comfortable using a range of characters in his comedies, from beggars to kings and everyone in between. We are allowed to laugh at everyone in Shakespeare's plays, not just the poorer and more common people.

Shakespeare's comedies often comment on human nature and how funny it can be, and on the many obstacles that stand in the way of true love. Shakespeare has many different ways of commenting on these, most of them dating back to the ancient Greeks, such as using *pun*, *innuendo*, farce, satire, and slapstick.

PUN

A joke made by using the play of similar words or sounds.

INNUENDO

A comment, usually not complimentary, on another person's character that is not said outright but only hinted at. Innuendo is often used in comedy.

But probably the most important characteristic of Shakespeare's comedies is that they have happy endings. He finds a way to reassure us in the end that the chaotic world will come to order, that people can get along despite major differences, and that situations are never as bad as we think. At the end of one of these plays, you just know everything is going to be all right.

Small Group ACTivity

Act out the second half of the last scene of *Measure for Measure* in two ways: First, have Isabella accept the Duke's marriage proposal. Then, have Isabella reject the Duke's proposal. Discuss the differences. What interpretation does your audience like better? What effect does it have on the rest of the play? Which do you prefer as an actor?

Sources for Comedies

As we learned in chapter one, Shakespeare didn't just make up all the stories he wrote. His plays were often based on a story that the general public was already familiar with, and his comedies in particular were based on at least two or three different sources. This often made his plays more popular, as audiences liked seeing new versions of stories they had heard before. Of course, Shakespeare didn't simply make popular stories into plays. He picked and chose what he wanted to include from the original source, leaving out the boring and superfluous stuff and keeping (although sometimes changing) the useful stuff. How he used or changed the source material depended upon what kind of play he was writing. Let's look at the source material for *A Midsummer Night's Dream* and see how it changed into a classic Shakespearean comedy.

Chaucer's *Canterbury Tales*

Geoffrey Chaucer's *Canterbury Tales* was one of the first works to be written in English, although if you were to read the original text it would be difficult to understand, as it was written in Middle English. Written at the end of the 1300s, the *Canterbury Tales* is a collection of stories told by various people on a ***pilgrimage*** to the English city of Canterbury, where there was (and still is) a famous and beautiful cathedral. Shakespeare was familiar with the *Tales*, and he used several of Chaucer's plots and characters in his own stories, sometimes even combining them.

PILGRIMAGE

A religious person's journey to a special and meaningful shrine or sacred place.

The first of the *Canterbury Tales* is called *The Knight's Tale*. The knight tells a story about a king in the ancient Greek city of Athens named Theseus, who goes to war against the Amazons, conquers them, and marries their queen, Hippolyta. After another battle, he imprisons two princes, who see a girl, Hermia, from their prison window and fall in love with her. The two princes are eventually freed, and as soon as they meet again, they begin to fight over Hermia. One of the princes dies, and Hermia marries the other after a period of mourning.

While *The Knight's Tale* ends tragically, Shakespeare alters it so that order is restored and the story ends happily, complete with the trademark wedding (or in this case, weddings). In Shakespeare's version, Theseus and Hippolyta are not yet married—that's saved for the comedy's happy ending. Shakespeare also uses the story of the lovers, but changes it somewhat: Because Chaucer's story lacks the truly happy ending that a good comedy needs, Shakespeare adds another woman (Helena) so that neither of the knights has to die and both can be happily married at the end.

Puck

Shakespeare's audiences were already familiar with the mischievous character Puck. Puck is just one name for a magical ***imp*** who makes trouble. He appears in the folklore of many countries, including Sweden, Ireland, and Greece. In fact, many people probably believed Puck was a real being, blaming him whenever their food rotted or their crops went bad. At the time Shakespeare wrote *A Midsummer Night's Dream*, there

IMP

A mischievous and sometimes evil sprite or spirit, usually found in folklore.

weren't any specific stories actually written down about Puck—he was more like an urban legend, and everybody had their own version. So the obnoxious pranks that Puck pulls in the play are not necessarily documented in any other literature, but they were believable nonetheless to audiences because they are the sort of things an evil imp would do.

Puck's main function in *A Midsummer Night's Dream* is to emphasize a common theme in Shakespearean comedy: the folly of human nature. In fact, Puck even comes out and says it: "Lord, what fools these mortals be!" (Act III, Scene ii, Line 115). Even though he is a trickster, all he really has to do is exploit the desires and emotions that humans feel already. Not being human himself, he is in the perfect position to laugh at the petty foibles and dramas of humanity and to encourage us to laugh with him.

Solo ACTivity

Many of Shakespeare's plays were based on popular, well-known stories or parts of history. If he were writing today, what stories would he use? Write a scene from a "current" Shakespeare play based on a popular, well-known story such as an urban legend, popular movie, or news item. Don't forget to give your new play a name! **Large Group Variation:** Act out the scene from the "new" Shakespeare play for an audience, then discuss with them how it compared to the original story and what kind of artistic license you took.

Ovid's *Metamorphoses*

While it seems that the characters of Bottom and the rude mechanicals came straight from Shakespeare's imagination, the play they put on for the wedding at the end, *Pyramus and Thisbe*, has its origins in the poetry of a Roman poet named Ovid. He tells the story of two young lovers, Pyramus and Thisbe, who live next door to each other but whose parents have forbidden them to see each other. Instead, they find a chink in the dividing wall to talk through late at night, and they finally decide to meet in a nearby graveyard. Thisbe gets there first and sees a lioness drinking at a nearby stream. The lioness has just killed and eaten an ox, and is therefore covered with blood; Thisbe is so scared that she runs to a nearby cave, dropping her scarf. The lioness tears and bloodies the scarf and leaves. When Pyramus finds Thisbe's bloody scarf, he assumes the blood is hers and holds himself accountable for her death. He draws his sword and kills himself in his misery. Thisbe creeps out of her cave and finds Pyramus dying on the ground; seeing the scarf, she realizes what has happened and uses the same sword to kill herself.

You might wonder what a sad story like this is doing in a Shakespearean comedy. There are two main functions: First, the way the silly actors portray it in this play-within-a-play is much less tragic than the original, making the characters that much more funny. Secondly, the tragic ending of *Pyramus and Thisbe* offsets the happy ending of *A Midsummer Night's Dream*, so that we appreciate it that much more.

Solo ACTivity

Write a short story of your own based on the story of Pyramus and Thisbe. Would you choose to modernize it at all? What misunderstandings will you create to lead up to a tragic, ironic conclusion? Could you instead create misunderstandings to lead up to a comic conclusion? Read your finished story and the original *Pyramus and Thisbe* again, and make notes on the comparison. What parts of the original story did you keep? What did you change, and why?

SHAKESPEARE'S TRAGEDIES

When classifying Shakespeare's plays, there always seems to be some debate. Some people would rather put Shakespeare's tragedies and history plays all into one category, and call them all tragedies. But since we are also looking at the source material Shakespeare used in writing his plays, we will make the distinction between tragedies and histories. Therefore, for our purposes, the plays that fall into the category of tragedy are as follows:

Titus Andronicus

Romeo and Juliet

Julius Caesar

Hamlet

Othello

King Lear

Macbeth

Timon of Athens

Antony and Cleopatra

Coriolanus

What's In a Name?

The first major difference you'll notice between Shakespeare's comedies and his tragedies is how he named the plays. For the comedies, he chose names that suggested something of the storyline: The title *A Midsummer Night's Dream* invokes a magical world of the imagination, while *Much Ado About Nothing* suggests that, while there may be dramatic uproar about something that seems incredibly important at the time, it will turn out to be nothing but happiness in the end.

The titles of Shakespeare's tragedies, on the other hand, tend to be people's names. There are several reasons for this. First, many of the plots of his tragedies were pulled from actual history, in which case Shakespeare's audience would know something about the ending just by hearing the name of the main character, without his having to allude to the plot. So he was banking on name recognition: Elizabethan audiences would know who Antony and Cleopatra were, for example, and would therefore be interested in seeing a play about them. Secondly, because they were pulled from history, Shakespeare had less of a tendency to combine several sources into one play, and to use them as they were rather than changing them so much. Thirdly, the title of a play often read something like *The Tragedy of Macbeth*, and that's pretty much all you had to know. As mentioned before, when it's a tragedy, you know that everybody dies in the end, so there would be no reason to name *Macbeth* something more suggestive of the plot, such as *The Deadly Consequences of Ambition*; that would be overstating it. Best simply to use the name of the main character, mention that it's a tragedy, and let the audience come see the play if they want to know more.

Small Group ACTivity

Look at a list of Shakespeare's tragedies and histories, then make up your own alternative titles for some or all of them. Try naming them more like the comedies are named, with phrases that allude to the story line. Once you have made your alternative title list, share with the others in your group. Are any of them similar? How are they different?

Death and Chaos

It is wrong to assume that absolutely *everybody* dies at the end of a tragedy. In fact, what makes tragedies so sad is that there are often a few people left behind, who then have to find a way to start over. It is often difficult because the **protagonist**, or main character, always dies, and since the protagonist is often a great leader, such as a prince or a general, it is difficult to know how to proceed in the chaos that follows. It would be as if the President, the Vice President, the whole Cabinet, and everyone else in the line of succession died at the same time—we would be left to try and figure out how to make order out of the chaos again and decide who should lead us in that direction.

> **PROTAGONIST**
>
> Usually the main character in a play, who drives the action, or around whom the action is centered.

Tragic Flaw

Another major characteristic of Shakespeare's tragic heroes is that they almost always have a major flaw, often referred to as a **tragic flaw**, which becomes their undoing in the end. That's another thing that's so sad about watching tragedy: It makes you wish you could go up to the protagonist and shake him, saying "Do you realize you're doing this to YOURSELF? Stop it!" Macbeth's tragic flaw is his ambition, because once he finally gets to the top, he thinks he's indestructible, and that's what gets him in the end. King Lear's tragic flaw is pride, which causes him to banish the only one of his three daughters who truly loves him and would have taken care of him in his old age.

> **TRAGIC FLAW**
>
> A personality trait in a tragic hero which leads him or her to make poor decisions resulting in tragic consequences. Tragic flaws often cause the character to be his own undoing.

Fickle Finger of Fate

Protagonists' flaws aren't the only thing that makes a tragedy tragic, however. There is still the important element of doom, or **fate**, or destiny—whatever you want to call it. This is an ancient concept. If a character is doomed to die, nothing he does will save him.

> **FATE**
>
> A universal force which can determine the course of the lives of human beings. Used as a literary device, fate often works against or in spite of the free will of the characters.

On the one hand, then, there is all this awful carnage that could have been prevented if the protagonist would just wake up and stop his own self-destructive behavior. And on the other hand, it is very sad to realize that these horrible events cannot be stopped at all, and no matter what the protagonist does, he is just a pawn in fate's game.

The Appeal of Tragedy

So you'd think, after all this, that no one would ever want to watch a tragedy. Then why are the tragedies some of Shakespeare's most popular plays? For one thing, they're amazing character studies. Remember that they were written in a time before modern psychology, and yet Shakespeare manages to show us the inner turmoil of the human mind in a way no other dramatist can. When it comes right down to it, as a society, we're all interested in how people behave under different types of pressure. Hence the recent onslaught of "reality TV," in which everyday people are put into extreme situations while we watch. Shakespeare does nearly the same thing: His tragedies are a study of how characters behave under extreme circumstances, with very high stakes—the character must prevail or the kingdom will be lost, someone will die, or a murderer will go unpunished, for example.

If Shakespeare's comedies explore humanity's capacity for goodness, the tragedies certainly examine all the possibilities of human malice, evil, greed, and prejudice. Although they are not meant to be outright lessons, they certainly do teach us about all the horrible things that can result from giving in to our basest tendencies. Shakespeare showed that violence and dishonesty can never solve our problems.

The "Rules" of Tragedy

Before Shakespeare started writing tragedies, there were some strict rules already in place—even more than for comedy. Again, the rules originated in Ancient Greece, this time from the pen of a philosopher named Aristotle. He wrote a treatise called the *Poetics*, in which he listed all the proper elements of tragedy. For one thing, Aristotle believed that the protagonists in a tragedy should be royalty. Such important and heavy decisions as tragic heroes must make should be the domain of the high-born, while the lighter, more trivial stuff of comedies should be left to more common, low-born characters.

The other major elements of tragedy that Aristotle insisted upon were the **unities**. He believed that, in order to be a good tragedy, there must be unity of

UNITIES

Dramatic rules, originating from the Greek writer Aristotle, that require that a play should concern a single action and should take place in one setting on one day. These are called the unities of action, place, and time.

time, unity of place, and unity of action. Unity of time suggests that the action of the play must take place in one day—whatever the issue is, it must be resolved in one 24-hour period, and cannot be drawn out into days, weeks, months, or years. Unity of place is just what it sounds like: All the action had to happen in one place. If you think about it in terms of staging, a play with unity of place wouldn't need any scene changes. Unity of action is a little more abstract—for the most part, it means that the play should only show one action, leaving no room for subplots.

You can see that Shakespeare didn't follow very many of Aristotle's rules, and when he did, it was only because they would serve his purposes. For instance, many of Shakespeare's tragic protagonists happen to be royalty, such as Prince Hamlet and King Lear. But Romeo and Juliet are just a couple of everyday kids, Othello is a general, and Macbeth's whole problem is that he's *not* a king (at least, not to begin with). It is the fact that Macbeth wants to become royalty that gets him into trouble.

As for the unities, Shakespeare ignored them completely. Many of his tragedies take place over the course of a few days, but certainly none of them occur within one 24-hour period, so unity of time is not followed. Unity of place is also dropped, as even *Hamlet*, most of which happens in the castle of Elsinore, takes place in several different rooms, not to mention the graveyard where Ophelia is buried and a ship bound for England. And there have been actual maps made of all the places in Verona where *Romeo and Juliet* takes place. As for unity of action, that can be dismissed at once when one considers all of Shakespeare's subplots; there is always more than one story happening in a Shakespeare play.

Sources for Tragedies

Many of Shakespeare's tragedies came from history and popular stories. Some were events that really did take place, and some were legends that may have taken place and were finally written down from their oral traditions. *Hamlet* originates from one of these stories.

The character Hamlet may have once been a real person, but we have no way of knowing because his story was told orally for so long that the details might have changed completely. The story was told for hundreds of years before a historian named Saxo Grammaticus wrote a history of Denmark in 1185.

Amleth, Prince of Denmark is only part of Saxo's whole work, but Shakespeare follows it pretty closely, right down to the title. Aside from making Hamlet's name easier for English people to pronounce, Shakespeare didn't change a thing, thereby solidifying what we already know about the titles of tragedies: they're often just people's names. He could have called it something like *Blood Revenge Upon a Usurper,* but that would sound more like the title of a comedy.

Shakespeare followed Saxo's story pretty closely, with a couple of exceptions: He shortened it a bit (he took out some of Saxo's unnecessary scenes at the end), and he made some changes that render it a more Shakespearean tragedy.

For instance, Saxo specifically mentions that Amleth *pretends* to be stupid and crazy, because he is worried that his uncle will kill him next. In Shakespeare's version, however, he leaves us wondering whether Hamlet is merely pretending to go crazy as a ruse to keep his mother and uncle off balance, or whether it's all just too much for him and he really is losing his mind.

Shakespeare's treatment of this situation has two important consequences: First, it introduces the tragic flaw, which in Hamlet's case is indecision. He is paralyzed by it, and by the time he gets up enough courage to kill Claudius, too many people have already died, including Hamlet's own mother. Secondly, Saxo's version pretty much takes away the possibility of fate's hand. If Amleth just "pretends" to be crazy, then he is still in complete control of the events in the play, whereas Shakespeare's Hamlet is fate's pawn from the beginning, unable to make his own decisions, which makes us sympathetic toward him. We are left thinking that if the universe had just been a bit kinder to him, these awful things may not have happened.

Ophelia, Hamlet's girlfriend, doesn't have a name in Saxo's version, and her involvement in the story isn't nearly as large. But Shakespeare lets Ophelia become a classic example of another characteristic of tragedy: how people behave under extreme circumstances. It is so sad to watch Ophelia's mind come unhinged as she endures the death of her father and brother and the breakup with Hamlet. She is put under enormous pressure, and she breaks. Her subsequent suicide lends yet another tragic note to an already tragic play.

Shakespeare enriches Saxo's story with more of his own inventions, such as Laertes' friendship and the "play within a play" that depicts Claudius as the murderer of Hamlet's father. Shakespeare also ties up the end of the story more neatly, making Claudius more of an instrument of Hamlet's downfall.

All in all, Shakespeare's version of the story of the Prince of Denmark is much more psychological and therefore more tragic, and adds the classic tragic concepts of fate, tragic flaw, death, and chaos.

Small Group ACTivity

Choose a Shakespeare play and try to find the actual history, myth, or story the play is based on. Choose part of the story to act out, then perform the corresponding scene of the play that is based on it. Discuss similarities and differences with your classmates. What parts of the original source did Shakespeare change? What stayed the same? What did he leave out or add in? **Variation:** Do the same exercise with a Shakespeare play and another play or story that is based on it, such as *Romeo and Juliet* and Leonard Bernstein's *West Side Story.* How does it compare to Shakespeare's story? What are the similarities and differences?

SHAKESPEARE'S HISTORIES

Even thought they are also tragedies, the history plays are placed in a separate category because Shakespeare took their plots from actual English history. In a way, he was writing about his own heritage, and his audiences loved it. All of the history plays are about great (or sometimes evil) English kings, and while it's true that he used the basic framework that historians of the time had written down, he did change some of the details to suit his own dramatic purposes. Here is a list of Shakespeare's history plays:

Henry VI, Part I

Henry VI, Part 2

Henry VI, Part 3

Richard III

Richard II

King John

Henry IV, Part 1

Henry IV, Part 2

Henry V

Henry VIII

When you hear the words "history play," you may thing they're just a boring list of events from the past. But Shakespeare uses history as a jumping-off point. He explores a lot of issues, like whether a ruler is actually ordained by God, and what characteristics make a truly effective king. He also uses history for great character studies, getting inside the minds of the great rulers and portraying the emotional turmoil that the rulers must have gone through while leading their people. Shakespeare's history plays are not just royal propaganda. Even though the main characters are all royalty, he shows that even kings can be fallible and weak. He examines the corruptive effects of power and greed. He lets us see that being king isn't all it's cracked up to be.

The history plays also have some humor in them. As we learned before, tragedies sometimes have some comedy in them, and Shakespeare uses the funny parts to introduce some of the more everyday characters, such as knights, servants, and innkeepers. These scenes also show us that what happens to royalty affects everyone else as well.

The "Rules" of Histories

For the most part, the structure and characteristics of Shakespeare's histories are much the same as for his tragedies. The main difference is that, for the histories, Shakespeare happens to follow Aristotle's rule that says the main characters must be royalty. But the main reason for this is that the history plays are based on…well, history, and in Shakespeare's day that meant the history of kings. In other words, when a historian in Shakespeare's time decided to write down any part of history, he would do so in terms of what the king or queen was doing at the time. It would never occur to a historian of Shakespeare's time to write down the history of a common, everyday person. That is a relatively new concept. So when Shakespeare decided to base a play on history, the only source material he had to work with was the history of kings—and therefore, kings became his main characters.

The Elizabethans did not view history the way we do in the 21st century. We believe that historians should portray events in the past as *objectively* as possible, which means we don't want them to insert their own opinions, prejudices, or political philosophy. We just want the facts so that we can decide for ourselves.

But Shakespeare didn't seem concerned with following his source material exactly. This means that when you see one of Shakespeare's history plays, you

ARTISTIC LIBERTY

The freedoms that artists (such as writers, performers, and directors) take with the truth or original material. Sometimes an artist adjusts material to make it more interesting or compelling to watch or read.

aren't seeing events as they actually happened. It's not like watching a documentary. Instead, the basic framework of what you are seeing is most likely accurate, but Shakespeare changed details as he saw fit, mostly because he wanted his plays to be interesting and exciting to watch. This is called taking *artistic liberty*.

This distinction also applies to plays and movies. Consider a couple of recent films about World War II (see, we still like war stories): *Schindler's List* and *Band of Brothers* (an HBO miniseries). The point of these projects was to faithfully recreate the background, circumstances, and experiences of the people who lived through those times.

Compare this approach with that of another movie, *Amadeus*, about the life of the composer Mozart. One of Mozart's rivals had once said: "I killed Mozart."

The rival was speaking metaphorically, saying that he had killed Mozart's career, but the writer of *Amadeus* decided to interpret this declaration literally, because he wanted to write a story about jealousy and its terrible consequences. He had something he wanted to say, which was more important to him than simply relating the facts, so he took artistic liberty. Shakespeare took the same approach when he wrote *Richard III*. He had something he wanted to say about political corruption, power, and mankind's lust for it.

Solo ACTivity

Choose a scene from one of Shakespeare's tragedies or histories and rewrite it, taking out all the conflict. What happens to the plot? Would the play be shorter or longer if all the conflict was missing? Would it be interesting to watch? What effect does conflict have on the plots of plays? **Scene Suggestions:** *Romeo and Juliet,* Act III, Scene i; *Othello,* Act IV, Scene i; *King Lear,* Act I, Scene i.

Sources for Histories

Although *Richard III* is a "history" play, it didn't seem like ancient history to Shakespeare and his audiences. The events actually took place only about 100 years before the play's first performance, so the story would have been known to the London public of the 1590s—in much the same way as you would know stories about World War I or the American West.

TETRALOGY

A set of four literary works (such as plays) whose stories run in succession. Like a trilogy, but with one more.

THE WARS OF THE ROSES

The battles for the throne of England between the families of Lancaster and York, whose family emblems were a red rose and a white rose, respectively.

Richard III is the concluding play in a *tetralogy* of plays about *the Wars of the Roses*, which were the battles for the throne of England between the families of Lancaster and York. The first three plays in the tetralogy are *King Henry VI Parts I, II, and III.* Shakespeare's audiences would have enjoyed the plays in exactly the same way as you would enjoy a series like *Lord of the Rings* or the *Star Wars* movies. Shakespeare's audiences not only knew the story of Richard III, but they really looked forward to it as the final episode of an exciting series.

But if they knew the story, what exactly did they know? Did they really have the facts, or was it just gossip, passed on by word-of-mouth? Or was it more sinister, being used as political propaganda? And did Shakespeare know any better than his audiences? And was it even possible that his character was not based on historical truth at all, but on other theatrical characters that had appeared on the English stage throughout the 16th century? Let's look at where Shakespeare actually learned the stories.

Shakespeare's play, *Richard III*, was based on one source in particular, *The Chronicles of England, Scotland, and Ireland*, written in about 1587 by a man named Raphaell Holinshed. In turn, Holinshed based his *Chronicles* on the work of a man named Edward Hall, who wrote *The Union of the Two Noble and Illustrious Families of Lancaster and York*. Hall's work was based on Sir Thomas More's *The History of King Richard the Third*. So you could say that Shakespeare's *Richard III* was based on all three of these works.

Shakespeare got most of his facts from Hall and Holinshed, but he derived the idea that Richard was a crafty, calculating, ruthless, but somehow charming villain from Sir Thomas More. More was not worried about creating something factually accurate. He was quite content to create something that was more like a work of art. He saw himself as an interpreter or commentator, not as a journalist.

But can we be sure that Sir Thomas More *did* distort things? There are some pretty convincing clues. For instance, portraits of King Richard show that he was actually quite a handsome fellow, perhaps with one shoulder a little lower than the other. It was More who reported that Richard had a humped shoulder, a spindly arm and a gross mouth. And if you really think about it, Henry VII actually had much better reasons for killing the Princes in the Tower than Richard, whose claim to the throne was a better one.

But if the "villainous Richard" was actually a creation of Tudor propaganda, how much was Shakespeare aware of that, and how much did he willingly participate in it? Because Shakespeare was a pretty smart guy, we can rest assured that he understood the distortions built into his sources. As we have already said, he wanted to write something about power and its pursuit. Nonetheless, there must also have been *something* of a political realist in him. Since Queen Elizabeth (who, as we know, was ruling when Shakespeare wrote the play) was a Tudor and a descendent of Henry VII, it really would not have been smart at all to write a play that would offend her by praising Richard. So it was probably quite convenient for Shakespeare to write Richard's story from this particular angle.

But Shakespeare didn't just adopt the changes to history made by others. He made plenty of his own. Let's look at just two examples. First, Shakespeare altered the timeline of events. The play shortens history. It begins with Henry VI's funeral. Shortly afterward, King Edward dies. This actually took more than 10 years—but clearly it would be dramatically less interesting to separate these events by such a period of time.

Second, Shakespeare also fleshed out the historical characters, but always with a purpose in mind. For instance, at the beginning of Act III, he portrays the boy King Edward V as asking pertinent questions about history. Shakespeare wanted to show us that Edward would have been a worthy king. But there is no historical documentation to suggest what Edward was really like. This is Shakespeare's invention to add to his overall interpretation.

Small Group ACTivity

Compare the Richards. When the great English actor, Laurence Olivier, portrayed Richard in a film way back in the 1940s, his portrayal of Richard as a grotesque villain somehow became the true Richard III in everyone's mind. But another great English actor, Ian McKellen, did a film version of the play set in Nazi Germany of the 1930s. Watch both movies and discuss the actors' choices. Why do you think each chose to portray Richard the way they did? How does each performance make you feel about King Richard III? Which do you think was more effective, and why? What are the differences and similarities between the two Richards?

SHAKESPEARE'S ROMANCES
AND PROBLEM PLAYS

Some people prefer to lump all of the *romances* and problem plays into the "comedy" category and have done with it, but this particular group of plays has some distinct differences from Shakespeare's conventional comedies. As a general rule, the romances and problem plays are considered to be the following:

ROMANCES

A literary genre characterized by adventurous and epic plots, characters, and settings.

Troilus and Cressida

All's Well That Ends Well

Measure for Measure

Pericles

Cymbeline

The Winter's Tale

The Tempest

The Two Noble Kinsmen

The major characteristics of the problem plays are that they deal with—you guessed it—problems, specifically those of a social or moral nature. Of course, all of Shakespeare's plays do this to a certain extent, but in the problem plays, Shakespeare seems particularly troubled by them. He cannot laugh them off or tie them neatly up with a fifth-act wedding, as he does in the comedies, and he cannot use them as a lesson or a catalyst for change as he does in the tragedies and histories.

It is for this reason that the problem plays get their other definition: They are a problem to understand and interpret. Shakespeare leaves more for us to decide, almost asking us to do our own moral self-examination as we watch the characters flounder for a way to solve their problems. Problem plays are not produced as often as the other types of plays, often for this reason. Directors are sometime unsure how to interpret them, and they're worried that audiences will just leave the theatre confused rather than enlightened or entertained.

The romance plays are also not produced very often, with the possible exception of *The Tempest*. The fact that they are called "romances" may be misleading; the term has less to do with plot and more to do with style. In modern-day terms, the word "romance" has become synonymous with love, but historically, to call a story "romantic" meant that it was less realistic than fantastic, that it went to emotional extremes, and that it was epic and adventurous in scope. Shakespeare's romances have characters that are more flamboyant and unusual, settings that are more imaginative and fictitious, and plots that are more unlikely than his other comedies. They are more like fairy tales.

The "Rules" of Problem and Romance Plays

The rules for this category are…that there are no rules! Most of these plays were written later in Shakespeare's career, when he was very likely feeling more adventurous and cynical than he'd been in his youth.

Although these plays have major themes and issues in common, there is no sort of structure that Shakespeare follows. The problem plays, for instance, are often resolved much like the comedies are, with weddings at the end. But at a problem-play wedding, not everyone looks happy to be there. You will find yourself thinking, "This wedding isn't a good idea—the marriage is never going to last." It's almost as though Shakespeare is mocking the idea of a happy ending.

The problem plays address such issues as justice and mercy, look at the lengths that human beings will go to in order to get what they want, and question whether traditional institutions, such as marriage, are always the best choice for everyone. In the problem plays, Shakespeare's good characters don't always turn the other cheek, and his bad characters don't always get what's coming to them. Problem plays are more likely to leave conflicts open-ended.

For instance, at the end of *Measure for Measure*, the Duke proposes to Isabella. You would think this was a good thing, but it actually presents a big problem for her, because she is preparing to become a nun and takes her vows very seriously. In addition, she has just proven that she would rather let her brother die than give up her chastity to the evil man who wants to kill him. So just when things are resolved and the Duke has put everything right on her behalf, he suddenly decides that he is more important than other men, her religion, and her convictions, and that she'll drop everything and marry him. But here's the amazing thing: Isabella doesn't answer him. Shakespeare didn't write any lines for her that respond to the Duke's proposal. This means that the director or the actress playing Isabella can decide whether she actually accepts the Duke's proposal (by silently taking his hand) or rejects it (by silently turning away). Shakespeare has left the conflict unsolved, and looks to us to solve it. No wonder it's called a "problem play"!

The romance plays, on the other hand, involve fewer moral dilemmas than the problem plays. They often involve such subject matter as shipwrecks, magic, fairies, princesses, and the separation and reunion of families. Shakespeare used Greek myth as the source for his romances more than any of his other plays, which is why they are so epic in nature. Greek myths often involve long journeys, joyful reunions, mysterious monsters, and imaginary worlds. As a result of this, a lot of what goes on in the romances is very unlikely, so they may sometimes seem harder to believe than Shakespeare's other comedies and tragedies. But this also makes them more joyful and childlike.

In *The Tempest*, for example, Prospero and his daughter Miranda are shipwrecked on an island. Prospero becomes a powerful magician, who can even control the weather. He stirs up a powerful, violent storm to set the events of the play in motion, and later on we see that his magic is so powerful, he can control people and enslave spirits. It's not particularly realistic, but it's still fun to watch and does teach us about jealousy, love, and power.

Like Shakespeare's regular comedies, the romances express a basic belief in humanity. The difference in the romances is that Shakespeare goes to greater, more fantastic lengths to solve the problems that the humans create.

REVIEWING THE FOUR TYPES

As you have learned, the four types of Shakespeare's plays do have elements in common. But at the same time, they all have characteristics that make them unique. You may have a favorite genre, or you might like them all equally.

Below is a Venn diagram to help you picture the similarities and differences more clearly. As you can see, each circle is devoted to one type of play. The points where the circles intersect contain their common characteristics, and the point where they all intersect in the center indicates elements common to all of Shakespeare's plays.

THE FOUR TYPES OF PLAYS:
A VENN DIAGRAM

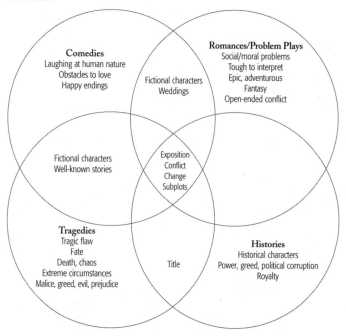

Comedies
Laughing at human nature
Obstacles to love
Happy endings

Romances/Problem Plays
Social/moral problems
Tough to interpret
Epic, adventurous
Fantasy
Open-ended conflict

Fictional characters
Weddings

Fictional characters
Well-known stories

Exposition
Conflict
Change
Subplots

Tragedies
Tragic flaw
Fate
Death, chaos
Extreme circumstances
Malice, greed, evil, prejudice

Title

Histories
Historical characters
Power, greed, political corruption
Royalty

Small Group ACTivity

Using a Shakespeare play you are familiar with, match it to its type in the Venn diagram above. Then, make a list of plot points, subject matter, and characters that make the play you have chosen fall into that category. What does it have in common with other plays you know? Does your play have any characteristics that make it different from the elements listed in the category? Discuss these points with your group.

❦ CHAPTER FOUR ❦

SHAKESPEARE'S CHARACTERS: STRONG WOMEN, TRAGIC HEROES, AND EVIL VILLAINS

O, wonder!
How many goodly creatures are there here!
How beauteous mankind is! O brave new world,
That has such people in 't.
—*The Tempest*, ACT V, SCENE I, LINES 215–218

CHARACTER TYPES

When we examine Shakespeare's characters to see what makes them tick, it is useful to group them into types for the sake of comparison. Unfortunately, there is not room to list and study them all, so we'll have to narrow it down to the most major and obvious groups. In this chapter, we'll discuss the following character types:

- Strong Heroines
- "Boy" Girls
- Ingénues
- Tragic Heroes
- Evil Villains
- Fools and Clowns

We'll look at the major characteristics of each type, and then get to know some of the specific characters that fall into each category.

When we talk about character types in the context of Shakespeare, however, it is important to realize that he didn't just use "stock" characters. When you think of a villain, for instance, what often comes to mind is a character in a black cape with oily dark hair and a moustache that curls at the ends, who has a name like "Snidely Whiplash" and goes around tying pretty girls to railroad tracks just for the fun of it. Those cartoonish villains are two-dimensional; they are evil simply for the sake of being evil. Shakespeare's villains, on the other hand, have *reasons* for being evil. They sometimes even feel the need to justify their evil deeds to the audience in the form of a soliloquy. They feel love, jealousy, embarrassment, and pain, and these feelings drive them to do horrible things. Shakespeare's villains, like his other characters, are three-dimensional.

During his writing career, Shakespeare created hundreds of characters, and somehow managed to endow each character with its own unique voice. This is no small feat. Think of how tired you would get, conceiving a different personality for each individual character in 38 plays! And yet, he did it so effectively that, to this day, people are still familiar with them and eager to share in their joy, pain, and laughter.

Shakespeare's characters are not just ideas who have a certain kind of job and live in a certain place and say certain witty things; they are well-rounded, three-dimensional human beings who wrestle with things like indecision, jealousy, and boundless hope. They are also dynamic characters who often change—sometimes for better, sometimes for worse—before our very eyes. As we watch, they make decisions that affect themselves and the world around them. You know that in real life, all people grow and change, sometimes over a period of years, sometimes over a period of days or weeks. Sometimes there is a catalyst for the change, such as the death of someone they love or a move to a new school or city. And you also know that sometimes relationships grow and change along with the changes in people, and sometimes they can't keep up. Sometimes friends have to stop being friends because one of them changes so much that the two are no longer compatible. Shakespeare knew all this too, and found a way to show it to us time and time again in his plays.

But, in this myriad of humanity that Shakespeare created, many of the characters have things in common with one another, and that is where we get the idea of character "types." It is by using these types that we will learn more about all of Shakespeare's characters.

Small Group ACTivity

Identify modern-day character types. For each category in this chapter, list characters from modern movies, television shows, books, and plays that match the characteristics. Name two or three characters for each category. You may also want to make a list of modern characters who "break the mold"—list those that don't fit into any category, and why. Or, you can make up your own character categories that fit modern characters better. Then, compare your list to those of the rest of your group. What did you agree on? What did you disagree on, and why?

Considerations for the Actor

Because there are distinct character types in Shakespeare, it might be easy to underestimate or oversimplify one when playing a role. It is important to remember that the role you are playing is not just a type, but a human being—and, as you probably already know, you can spend a lifetime getting to know a human being.

Some of Shakespeare's characters have very specific requirements in terms of casting. Helena from *A Midsummer Night's Dream* is spoken of as being tall, whereas her friend Hermia is short—so right there, that limits the number of actresses that could be cast in each role. Similarly, Falstaff is fat, thus requiring a similarly large actor. The twins from *Twelfth Night*, Viola and Sebastian, look enough alike that they are mistaken for one another; this would demand a pair of actors who looked enough alike that it would be believable.

The fact that Shakespeare's characters can be put into these categories means that actors can still be "typecast." For instance, although Lawrence Olivier played many of the brave men, tragic heroes, and evil villains, he never played Falstaff. Why? Because Olivier was never fat. Although he was a great actor, he could never have played Falstaff believably, because he simply didn't *look* like Falstaff. In fact, if you look at the resume of any actor, living or dead, who has played a lot of Shakespeare, you'll find that he or she has probably been cast in one or two different types, often corresponding to his or her physicality or age.

But aside from the practical considerations, there are many specific decisions that an actor is left to make on his own. Many of the best Shakespearean actors do this by having some sympathy for their characters. They try to understand why the character makes the decisions that he or she makes, even if the character is evil. And they often begin by trying to understand what type of character it is they are playing.

Solo ACTivity

Choose the character type that you think is most opposite of your personality (your choice doesn't have to match your gender). Choose a monologue or scene to perform for the class. Discuss whether it was harder or easier to play a character that was not at all like you. Ask the class whether it was convincing.

STRONG HEROINES

Many people believe that Shakespeare was a feminist (though, of course, this term didn't exist back in Shakespeare's lifetime), and when you look at some of his female characters, it is easy to see why. Many of Shakespeare's female characters are assertive, creative, intelligent people who do whatever it takes to right a wrong or to get what they want. They are able and willing to act on their own, although, in the end, their destiny usually gets tied in with a man's. It is possible that Shakespeare was simply reflecting Elizabethan beliefs which held that a woman's place was with her man, thus encouraging love and marriage for the female characters. But that doesn't usually happen until the end of the play, and in the meantime, we get to watch the women hatch amazing plots and assert themselves in the gravest of circumstances.

Shakespeare's heroines come from all walks of life. Sometimes they are the daughters of noblemen, sometimes serving maids or courtiers' daughters. During an era in which arranged marriages were still fairly common, Shakespeare's heroines often get to choose the person they fall in love with and eventually marry.

To learn more about Shakespeare's strong heroines, let's take a look at Portia from *Merchant of Venice*.

Portia

We actually hear about Portia before we meet her—and listening to what other characters say is a great way to learn about a character. In Act I, Scene i, Bassanio tells his buddy Antonio about Portia. The very first thing he says about her is that she's very wealthy because of an inheritance. He then mentions that she is blonde and beautiful and that he thinks she likes him because of the way she looks at him. The problem is that a lot of other people know that she's rich and available, so there are a lot of men competing for her attention. Here is Bassanio's speech. Read it and see if anything else stands out to you:

> *In Belmont is a lady richly left,*
> *And she is fair, and, fairer than that word,*
> *Of wondrous virtues: sometimes from her eyes*
> *I did receive fair speechless messages:*
> *Her name is Portia; nothing undervalued*
> *To Cato's daughter, Brutus' Portia:*
> *Nor is the wide world ignorant of her worth*
> *For the four winds blow in from every coast*
> *Renowned suitors: and her sunny locks*
> *Hang on her temples like a golden fleece*
> *Which makes her seat of Belmont Colchos' strond,*
> *And many Jasons come in quest of her.*
> *O my Antonio, had I but the means*
> *To hold a rival place with one of them,*
> *I have a mind presages me such thrift,*
> *That I should questionless be fortunate!*

Bassanio clearly thinks Portia is pretty great, but we have to keep in mind that he's also in debt up to his eyeballs. In fact, it sounds like most of the suitors are more interested in her money than in her. So even though Portia is beautiful, the fact that she's also rich seems to be her distinguishing feature to most of the men in her life.

When we meet Portia herself, she's with Nerissa, her maid and longtime companion, gossiping about men like any other girl. Interestingly, Shakespeare has Portia and Nerissa speaking in prose at this point, even though Portia is high born and well educated. The reason for this may be to emphasize the casualness of their conversation, because Portia is basically making fun of all the men who have come to seek her hand in marriage ("…there is not one among them but I dote on his very absence. And I pray God grant them fair departure! [Act I, Scene ii, Lines 109–111]). Portia definitely has a biting sense of humor and is not afraid to use it, but she is also very reasonable and logical. In his will, her dead father designed a way to choose a husband for her, and she is not allowed to marry someone in any other way. At the beginning of the scene she is upset about this, but at the end (after they finish privately insulting every ghastly suitor that has come her way), she has decided that her father's plan is actually a pretty good way of getting rid of most of the unwanted guys. Already, she has changed.

When Bassanio finally takes the casket test to win her hand in marriage in Act III, Scene ii, we really get a sense of Portia's integrity. She is an exceptionally honest human being. She tells Bassanio that she would like to tell him which is the right casket to choose (thereby ensuring that she'd get to marry him), but that would be going back on her word, and she doesn't want to do that. How many of us would stick to that? After all, her father is dead; if she breaks her promise to him, who would know besides she and Bassanio? And yet it is more important to her that she keep her word than that she marry the man she loves. She is willing to sacrifice a lifetime of happiness to preserve her integrity.

Fortunately, Bassanio picks the right casket after all, but then there is the problem of the money he has borrowed from Shylock in Antonio's name. If Shylock doesn't get his money back, he will kill Antonio. Portia sees it as her own responsibility to save Antonio's life, and takes it on herself to do whatever it takes to free him, not because she is in any way obligated to do so, but because she loves Bassanio, and she knows Bassanio loves his friend Antonio and would be crushed if anything happened to him.

It is at this point that Portia moves from being a young girl whose life is driven by the men in it, to being a woman who takes her life and the lives of others into her own hands. She stops being a pawn and starts being a player. For the first time she faces a problem that her money will not solve, and she rises to the occasion beautifully, realizing that she has to use her brains instead of her riches to save Antonio.

And here's where it gets interesting. Portia disguises herself as a man, a lawyer, and goes to the court where Antonio is being tried. She uses several different tactics to get Shylock to drop his charges; first she appeals to his vanity, suggesting that showing mercy gives one a great deal of power ("…it becomes the throned monarch better than his crown." [Act IV, Scene i, Lines 194–195]). But when he is not interested, she reminds him that he is being offered three times the amount of money he is owed ("Be merciful; Take thrice thy money; bid me tear the bond." [Act IV, Scene i, Lines 242–243]). When nothing else works, she tells him he is allowed to take the pound of Antonio's flesh that non-payment of the bond requires, but that he must not spill any blood ("But in the cutting of it, if thou dost shed one drop of Christian blood, thy lands and goods are by the laws of Venice confiscate…" [Act IV, Scene i, Lines 322–324]). Essentially, Portia has found a loophole. She shows us that she can be brave, smart, and incredibly clever.

To sum up Portia, we can safely say that she is driven to marry the right guy, but is very concerned for the welfare of others. She is resourceful and independent, yet comfortable giving control of her estate to Bassanio once she marries him, which shows that she is very confident in her choice of husband. She is respectful of tradition (letting her father decide how she should pick a mate), but isn't afraid to break the rules (disguising herself as a man). In the space of five acts, she is transformed from a giggling, gossiping girl into a smart, challenging woman who is in charge of her own destiny. She is indeed a strong heroine.

Describing Portia

Here is a list of adjectives and verbs that describe Portia. These might help you when studying her for a scene.

Adjectives	**Verbs**
Blonde	To give
Rich	To find (the right guy)
Loyal	To marry (Bassanio)
Funny	To seal (Bassanio's loyalty)
Honest	To save (Antonio)
Intelligent	To prove (that Shylock is wrong)
Beautiful	
Wise	
Generous	
Decisive	

Solo ACTivity

Make a description list for any character of your choosing. List the adjectives and verbs that best describe that character, both physically and psychologically, and using your list, decide what character category he or she belongs in. If you like, prepare a monologue or scene with the help of your description list.

Playing Portia

If you are interested in studying the role of Portia, you might want to start with these scenes and monologues.

Act I, Scene ii: two women (Portia and Nerissa)

Act III, Scene ii, lines 1–24: monologue (Portia speaking to Bassanio)

Act III, Scene ii, lines 42–64: monologue (Portia speaking to Bassanio, Nerissa, and the crowd)

Act III, Scene ii, lines 153–178: monologue (Portia speaking to Bassanio)

Act III, Scene iv, lines 63–81: monologue (Portia speaking to Nerissa)

Act IV, Scene i, lines 190–212: monologue (Portia speaking to Shylock)

"BOY" GIRLS

Shakespeare has a unique tendency to disguise his heroines as men, as we have already seen in Portia's case. But sometimes, they are disguised as men for most of the play, such as in *As You Like It* or *Twelfth Night*. In both cases, the girls disguise themselves to ensure their own survival while they try to figure out how to win the love of a man.

We have already discussed the possibility that Shakespeare was a feminist, or at least that he believed that women deserved more respect than they were given in his lifetime (with the notable exception of Queen Elizabeth). But the "boy" girls raise an interesting question. Perhaps Shakespeare is acknowledging that, in his world, one cannot get ahead unless one is a man, and these girls are simply smart enough to recognize that and do what it takes to get what they want. But he may also be saying that these girls simply aren't good enough, in their womanly form, to get ahead. Surely he had enough imagination to create a world in which a girl could get what she wants without having to disguise herself as a man. But we will never truly know, and in the meantime, we are left with the interesting phenomenon of strong female characters disguised as men, and all the advantages and comic pitfalls that such a disguise brings.

When it comes right down to it, Shakespeare's "boy" girls are crossdressers. Of course that expression didn't exist in Elizabethan times, but the fact is that they were challenging society's perception of gender roles. When dressed as men, Shakespeare's "boy" girls get to do the things only men got to do: go off on journeys by themselves, for instance, or choose husbands for themselves instead of having to have a father do it for them.

The crossdressing also makes the audience really think about the concepts of identity and self-perception. If you keep in mind the fact that all actors in Shakespeare's time were boys, then here is what you have: a boy, playing a girl, disguised as a boy. In *As You Like It* specifically, Rosalind helps Orlando (who thinks she is a boy named Ganymede) by pretending to be a girl so that he can practice saying all the nice things that he'd like to say to Rosalind. So in this case, you have a boy, playing a girl, disguised as a boy, pretending to be a girl. Are you confused yet?! Since we're discussing Rosalind specifically, let's take a look at her in greater detail.

Rosalind

When we first meet Rosalind in *As You Like It*, she is with her cousin Celia. Already this demonstrates a certain amount of maturity, because their fathers are enemies (even though they are brothers). But Rosalind and Celia never allow their fathers' antagonism to get in the way of their loyalty to one another; they are able to look beyond the politics of the court to maintain their friendship. Specifically, Celia's father, Duke Frederick, is angry over the disadvantages of being the younger brother to Rosalind's father, Duke Senior (such as not getting any of the family's land or riches). So he banishes Duke Senior to the Forest of Arden and takes over his castle, land, possessions, and title, but allows Rosalind to stay with Celia.

In this first conversation that we witness in Act I, Scene ii, Rosalind and Celia are speaking in prose instead of verse. As he does in many of his other plays, Shakespeare is using this to show how close and at ease Rosalind and Celia are with one another. They don't feel they have to put on the formality of speaking in metered verse when it's just the two of them.

When Rosalind and Celia finally meet Orlando, they all begin speaking verse. What's funny about this conversation, though—before and especially after the wrestling match—is that Orlando never has much to say. It is almost as if Rosalind is too much for him in the conversation department. She is so witty and articulate that it is hard for Orlando to dig up the confidence to meet her halfway.

The next time we see Rosalind, in Act I, Scene iii, the circumstances are much more serious. At first, she confesses to Celia that she has fallen in love with Orlando, and then Duke Frederick (Celia's father) walks in and banishes her from his court. He tells her that if she isn't out within ten days, he'll kill her.

At this shocking announcement, Rosalind shows us that she is not one to wallow in self-pity. Once Celia starts devising a plan to go into the Forest of Arden to find Duke Senior, Rosalind catches on to the optimism and begins adding her own ideas to the plan. It is Rosalind herself who decides to go disguised as a man, thus showing both practicality and bravery. She knows it is not safe for two girls to venture out into the woods together, and is willing to protect herself and Celia by becoming a man.

But Rosalind shows even more practicality when they get to the forest in Act II, Scene iv, because the first thing she does is buy a cottage, some land, and a flock of sheep. After all, a person has to have a place to live in the forest, right? Using Celia's jewels, Rosalind can buy property because she is now disguised as a man, Ganymede, and her natural practicality helps put her in charge of their affairs.

Once Rosalind meets up with Orlando again in Act III, Scene ii (and remember, she is in disguise as Ganymede now), she can be bold and strike up a real conversation with him. And since Orlando believes she is Ganymede, he is no longer tongue-tied, and is willing to tell her all about how he loves Rosalind. As their "friendship" develops further, Rosalind becomes worried that he isn't really in love with her, and that she must work harder as Ganymede to secure his feelings. She tells Orlando that she'll pretend to be Rosalind, so that he can learn how to woo her best. As she does this, she shows us a certain amount of self-knowledge. She doesn't fool herself into thinking she is always reasonable when it comes to love, and she assures Orlando of this. She is very honest and comfortable with herself and her own personality.

At the end of the play, Rosalind's natural optimism and resourcefulness allow her to orchestrate the ending that brings all the couples together in marriage and reunites her with her father, Duke Senior. And suddenly all is well again, as Duke Frederick has decided to give back to Duke Senior all that is rightly his, and everyone can return to court. We must remember that none of this would have happened without Rosalind—but it also could not have happened if she had tried to accomplish all of this as a female. It is only when she is disguised as Ganymede that she can take charge, own land, speak her mind, and take the initiative in their relationship with her future husband. But that doesn't seem to bother her at all, and she happily goes back to being a woman so that she and Orlando can get married.

Once the play is over, there's an additional treat: Rosalind gets an *epilogue*. But it is actually the actor playing Rosalind who speaks, and is so at ease with the audience that he (or, nowadays, she) speaks in prose. Once again we are confronted with gender issues, as the actor

> **EPILOGUE**
>
> A section, often performed by the actor himself, at the end of a play that sums up the play's action.

tells us it is unusual to for the epilogue to be done by a woman...but on the other hand, why not? Once again, we get to see Rosalind bucking tradition, adapting herself happily to the given situation and somehow making it all look very easy.

Describing Rosalind

Below is a list of adjectives and verbs that describe Rosalind's personality and actions.

Adjectives

Articulate
Versatile
Loyal
Tall
Beautiful
Brave
Resourceful
Optimistic
Intelligent

Verbs

To protect (herself and Celia)
To secure (Orlando's love)
To find (her father)
To buy (a place to live)
To organize events (so everyone is happy)

Playing Rosalind

Below is a list of scenes and monologues you might be interested in looking at if you want to play Rosalind. When Rosalind is in disguise as Ganymede, it is indicated.

Act I, Scene ii, lines 1–44: two women (Rosalind and Celia)

Act I, Scene iii: two women and one man (Rosalind, Celia, and Duke Frederick)

Act III, Scene i, lines 301–442: one man and one woman (Orlando and Rosalind as Ganymede)

Act III, Scene i, lines 414–431: monologue (Rosalind as Ganymede to Orlando)

Act III, Scene v, lines 39–69: monologue (Rosalind as Ganymede to Silvius and Phoebe)

Epilogue: soliloquy (the actor playing Rosalind to audience)

INGÉNUES

The last major category of female characters in Shakespeare is the ingénue. There is certainly some overlap between the three categories, but ingénues are, for the most part, younger and more naïve than heroines, and don't dress up as boys to get what they want. Ophelia in *Hamlet* and Juliet in *Romeo and Juliet* are two of Shakespeare's greatest and most famous ingénues.

Ingénues are often somehow bound up in their love for a boy, and the tragic ingénues often die in a way that is somehow connected with that boy. You might wonder if there is some sort of lesson in this—if Shakespeare is trying to tell young girls to protect their hearts and beware of boys. But even if that isn't Shakespeare's message, his ingénues show a touching tendency to believe completely in love and in their beloved, so that while they are young and sheltered, they are also brave.

Shakespeare's ingénues also wrestle with the issue of authority. Most of them truly want to obey the wishes of their parents (which are often along the lines of "Stay away from that boy!"), but conflict arises when they also try to follow their own hearts; they don't know how to please their parents and still be true to themselves. Sometimes circumstances beyond their control—often created by the very authority they are striving so hard to please—cut them off from all of their support. In Ophelia's case, this is especially destructive, as her only other means of support, her boyfriend Hamlet, has gone (or seems to have gone) crazy. So she finds herself very much alone in the world.

Ophelia is, indeed, one of Shakespeare's most fascinating characters, so let's take a look at her in more depth.

Ophelia

The first time Ophelia appears, she is with her brother Laertes as he finishes his packing in Act I, Scene iii. He is about to go away to France, and the very first things we hear him say to Ophelia, after he reminds her to write to him, are words of warning against Hamlet. Laertes knows Hamlet has expressed his love to Ophelia, and he's worried that Hamlet doesn't really mean it, or, if he does, that his feelings will only last a short time. The situation is further complicated, Laertes reminds her, by the fact that as prince of Denmark, Hamlet should really have his wife chosen for him, and Ophelia (because, we must assume, of her social standing) would not be the best choice to become Denmark's princess and eventual queen. Laertes finishes by telling her not to let down her guard.

This short scene alone shows us how very protected and sheltered Ophelia's life has been thus far. We never find out what happened to her mother, but it is clear that she has two men in her life, her father and her brother, who are very concerned for her well-being. Ophelia's reaction to her brother's speech, however, is funny, mostly because most of us know what it's like to feel overprotected ("You never let me do anything!"), and have reacted in a similar way. In this case, Ophelia tells Laertes to practice what he preaches.

The process starts all over again when their father, Polonius, enters. He makes her tell him what's going on between her and Hamlet, and reminds her that when a boy is physically attracted to a girl, he'll say just about anything, so she shouldn't believe him. He then forbids her to spend any more time with him. Ophelia, deciding (at least for now) to be the proper daughter, tells him, "I shall obey, my lord" (Act I, Scene iii, line 145).

The next time we see Ophelia, in Act II, Scene i, she is telling her father about a very disturbing encounter she has just had with Hamlet, in which he basically seemed crazy. Polonius assumes that Hamlet has gone insane because Ophelia has been refusing to see him, and rushes off to tell the King and Queen. What is interesting about this scene is that we as the audience never get to see the encounter she is describing—we only hear about it secondhand from her—so it may or may not be true. Maybe she's making it up, so that Polonius will decide it was a mistake not to let her see Hamlet anymore. Or maybe she and Hamlet conspired together, for the same reason. Or, maybe it really did happen and she is simply being honest and obedient by telling her father all about it right away. If she isn't telling the truth, however, she isn't as naïve as we had thought.

At this point, however, Ophelia becomes more of a political pawn for the King and Queen than anything else. They decide to use her to try to figure out what exactly is wrong with Hamlet, and Ophelia has no choice but to go along with the plan. So when she and Hamlet have an awful fight in which Hamlet says he never loved her, while her father and the King are watching secretly, Ophelia is positively crushed. Her line, "O, woe is me" (Act III, Scene I, line 174) says it all: Ophelia's safe, happy world is crumbling around her. To add insult to injury, after Hamlet leaves and the King and Polonius reappear to discuss his problem, neither of them consoles Ophelia or even acknowledges that she has just had her heart broken. It is as if she is an inanimate object.

But it is not until her father is killed—by Hamlet, no less—that Ophelia really loses it. Judging by what she says in Act IV, Scene v, she just can't handle the grief that her father's death has caused her, and instead loses touch with reality. But somehow in her depression she has gained a bit of wisdom. She says to the King, "Lord, we know what we are but know not what we may be" (Act IV, Scene v, lines 48–49), and we are left to wonder if she is speaking with hindsight of her own life: She knew she was happy, but never had any idea that she would ever be this sad.

After her "mad scene," we never see her again, and only hear of her death secondhand from the Queen as she tells Laertes. Gertrude tells us that, while Ophelia was picking flowers by the river, the branch she was leaning against broke and she fell in. We may wonder whether it was suicide or an accident that caused Ophelia's watery end, but Gertrude's interpretation of the situation is that Ophelia, being mad, was unaware of her peril, and therefore did nothing to try to save herself; however, it's also possible that Ophelia was very much aware that she might drown and simply didn't care.

Either way, we have witnessed a sweet, innocent girl move from a happy, safe childhood into a world of political deceit, romantic betrayal, and murder; and the change happens so quickly for her that, psychologically, she is simply unable to keep up. Being dumped by her boyfriend and losing her father were simply more than she could handle, and she is unable to pull herself out of the depression she spins into as a result.

Describing Ophelia

Here is a list of adjectives and verbs that describe Ophelia. These might help you when studying her for a scene.

Adjectives	Verbs
Sensitive	To love
Honest	To obey
Trusting	To protect (herself)
Manipulated	To escape (her grief)
Used	To understand (Hamlet)
Sweet	
Young	
Naïve	

Playing Ophelia

Here is a list of scenes and monologues from *Hamlet* that are useful for studying the role of Ophelia. The last two scenes listed are Ophelia's "mad scenes."

Act I, Scene iii, Lines 95–145: one woman, one man (Ophelia and Polonius)

Act II, Scene i, Lines 84–134: one woman, one man (Ophelia and Polonius)

Act III, Scene i, Lines 99–175: one woman, one man (Ophelia and Hamlet)

Act III, Scene i, Lines 163–175: soliloquy (Ophelia to audience)

Act IV, Scene v, Lines 26–78: two women, one man (Ophelia, Gertrude, Claudius)

Act IV, Scene v, Lines 178–225: one woman, one man (Ophelia and Laertes)

TRAGIC HEROES

The male characters that fall into the category of Shakespeare's "tragic heroes" are a little harder to define. When we talked about the genre of tragedy in chapter three, we learned that tragic heroes often have a tragic flaw that leads to their undoing, that they are often pawns of fate, and that they are under extreme circumstances.

That's just about all they have in common. Otherwise, Shakespeare's tragic heroes are very different from one another. Romeo, especially, stands out from the crowd because he is unusual. He is the youngest of all of them, and he is not royalty. But, like all tragic heroes, he dies needlessly at the end of the play, leaving those around him to try to get on with their lives.

Let's look at the highlights of Romeo's plight in a little more detail.

Small Group ACTivity

Switch the character types and see what happens. First, choose a scene between two clear character types, such as Hamlet and Ophelia. Perform the scene as if Ophelia were a strong woman rather than an ingénue, and as if Hamlet were an evil villain. How does it affect the scene and your portrayal of the character? Do the scene three times: once each changing only one character type at a time, and once changing both. **Variation:** Rewrite a character's lines to fit a different character type. Using the same example, keep Hamlet's lines the same, but rewrite Ophelia's responses as if she were a strong woman.

Romeo

Romeo will always be remembered as being bound in love to Juliet forever, but the funny thing is that, the first time we meet him in Act I Scene i, he is pining away for another girl named Rosaline. She is, he claims, the most beautiful creature he's ever seen, and he is despondent because she doesn't love him. So Romeo immediately establishes himself in our minds as a passionate person. In fact, it is rather startling to discover in Act I, Scene ii that the entire reason he sneaks into the Capulets' party (where he eventually meets Juliet) is because he hears Rosaline will be there. The other interesting thing about these two scenes is that Romeo is basing his feelings entirely on looks: Nowhere does he say that Rosaline is smart or witty or kind; and yet he decides he holds the deepest of affections for her because she is beautiful.

As Romeo and his friends are about to enter the party in Act I, Scene iv, Romeo mentions that he had a bad dream the night before and has a feeling that something will happen at the party that will start a horrible chain of events. He is right, of course; but does this make him extremely intuitive (or even psychic), or just depressed and pessimistic with an overactive imagination?

Much of the time, Romeo speaks in rhyming verse, which is impressive. From this we can conclude that he is very intelligent and cultured. When he first sees Juliet at the party, he speaks of her beauty in eloquent poetry. He is definitely a romantic, and his feelings are justified when Juliet falls in love with him immediately. He is charming and quite forward to her (he kisses her about 30 seconds after first meeting her), but she certainly doesn't seem to mind—and Romeo never brings up the subject of Rosaline again.

When Romeo and Juliet meet up again in Act II, Scene ii, Romeo is once again star-struck and dreamy, while Juliet is left to be the practical one. She is the one to bring up the fact that their families are mortal enemies. When she realizes he is on her father's property below her balcony, she immediately wants to know why and how he got there, and expresses concern that if he is found by any of the men in her family, they will kill him. But Romeo is completely unconcerned, and answers her questions with evasive and dreamy scraps of verse. Nonetheless, they decide to get married (only a few hours after having met!), and Romeo goes off to find the Friar, to persuade him to perform the marriage ceremony.

When Romeo finds the Friar in Act II, Scene iii, and tells him of his love for Juliet, the Friar expresses his confusion that Romeo was so recently in love with

Rosaline. Romeo answers him in such an offhand fashion that we almost believe he was not in the depths of depression over her just 24 hours earlier, but he does mention that Juliet is the better choice since she loves him back.

After Romeo and Juliet get married in secret, the feud between their families comes to a head when Romeo and his friends Benvolio and Mercutio meet up with Juliet's cousin Tybalt in the street in Act III, Scene i. This scene shows much of the two sides of Romeo's character. At first, he refuses to fight with Tybalt, because they are now kinsmen (now that Romeo and Juliet are married). Romeo's idealistic, romantic side shines through as he explains to Tybalt that if he only knew what had just happened (that is, the secret wedding), he wouldn't want to fight. But once Tybalt kills Mercutio, Romeo's passionate, impulsive side takes over, and he immediately kills Tybalt. And right away, he knows it is the beginning of the end for him: "This but begins the woe others must end" (Act III, Scene i, line125).

When we see Romeo next in Act III, Scene iii, he is almost hysterical at the news that the prince has chosen banishment over death as his punishment for Tybalt's murder. Friar Lawrence tries to explain that the prince was trying to be merciful by sparing him the death sentence, but Romeo is inconsolable: "'Tis torture and not mercy. Heaven is here where Juliet lives..." (Act III, Scene iii, lines 31–32). And it only gets worse from there. When Juliet's Nurse comes to tell Romeo how upset Juliet is over her cousin Tybalt's death, Romeo pulls his dagger and tries to stab himself with it, only to be stopped by the Friar. This is further evidence that Romeo's passionate, emotional tendencies can carry him too far. Indeed, even the Friar becomes impatient with Romeo's histrionics and scolds him: "Thy wild acts denote the unreasonable fury of a beast...by my holy order, I thought thy disposition better tempered" (Act III, Scene iii, lines 120–121 and 124–125).

Since the Friar allows Romeo one night with his new wife before his banishment, the next time we see Romeo is as he's about to leave Juliet's room the next morning. Interestingly, this is the only time where the tables are turned: Juliet is being dreamy and impractical, denying that morning has come, and Romeo has to remind her that if he doesn't leave soon, he'll be killed: "I must be gone and live, or stay and die" (Act III, Scene v, line 11). It is as if the sad reality of their situation is finally sinking in, and his dreamy optimism will no longer serve him.

But even to the last, Romeo remains beautifully articulate. In Act V, when he finds what he thinks is Juliet's dead body, his speech before taking the poison to join her in death is positively heartbreaking: "O, here will I set up my everlasting rest and shake the yoke of inauspicious stars from this world-wearied flesh!" (Act V, Scene iii, lines 109–112). It reminds us once again that Romeo never does anything halfway; whatever passion he finds, he throws himself into heart and soul, and when that passion is taken away, he truly believes he cannot live without it. Has he changed by the end of the play, or is he still the fickle youth who loved Rosaline at the beginning? If a girl more beautiful than Juliet or Rosaline had come along before he drank the poison, would Romeo have skipped his tragic demise and instead begun to passionately pursue a new "love of his life"?

But of course, we will never know, because instead we witness the end of his short life. In the way of a true tragic hero, Romeo does indeed have a flaw: his idealism. He is, if it is possible, too optimistic, especially when it comes to love, and it is this optimism that eventually causes his own demise. But like other tragic heroes, fate certainly has a hand in Romeo's story. We see fate's hand almost immediately in the form of the feud between the Capulets and the Montagues, as the prologue reminds us: "From forth the fatal loins of these two foes, a pair of star-crossed lovers take their life…" (prologue, lines 5–6). Romeo and Juliet are, in some respects, merely pawns in the greater battle between their families.

Describing Romeo

If you are interested in studying the character of Romeo in more depth, the following list of adjectives and verbs might help you to better define him.

Adjectives	Verbs
Idealistic	To marry (Juliet)
Romantic	To settle (the families' quarrel)
Dreamy	To avenge (Mercutio's death)
Impractical	To join (Juliet)
Passionate	To solve (the problem of their
Poetic	separation)
Capricious	To die (with Juliet)
Impulsive	
Optimistic	

> ### *Playing Romeo*
>
> If you are interested in playing the part of Romeo, here are some duets and monologues to help get you started:
>
> Act I, Scene i, lines 163–247: two boys (Romeo and Benvolio)
>
> Act II, Scene ii: one boy and one girl (Romeo and Juliet)
>
> Act II, Scene iv, lines 45–103: two boys (Romeo and Mercutio)
>
> Act V, Scene i, lines 37–60: soliloquy (Romeo to audience)
>
> Act V, Scene iii, lines 88–120: monologue (Romeo to the sleeping Juliet)

EVIL VILLAINS

Shakespeare's villains are some of his most fun and fascinating creations. The extent to which they can be entirely unscrupulous and conniving is simply amazing, not to mention the fact that they make us appreciate the nice people in Shakespeare's plays (and even in the world in general) all that much more.

One important thing to realize is that Shakespeare's villains are not evil simply for the sake of being evil. Not a single one of them wakes up in the morning and says to himself, "Hm, I think I'll be mean to people for the rest of my life." The difference between Shakespeare's good characters and his evil characters is the same as the difference between good people and bad people in real life. They both want something very badly, but the bad character is willing to hurt people or break laws or promises to get it, whereas the good character is not. So, Shakespeare's villains are simply people who have very specific goals and are immoral about achieving them, believing that the ends justify the means. Richard III, for instance, is one of Shakespeare's most famous villains. His major aspiration is to be king, and he has no scruples about killing whoever gets in his way (including his two nephews, who have the rights to the throne). He knows exactly what he wants and doesn't care what he has to do to get it.

Often, though, Shakespeare's villains end up being psychologically plagued as a direct result of the evil deeds they have done. Lady Macbeth, for instance, cannot escape the guilt she feels because of all the people she and her husband have killed just so he can become King of Scotland; it eventually drives her mad. Richard III ends up being visited by the ghosts of the people he has killed, whose curses cause him to lose the battle that ends in his own death.

To study Shakespeare's evil characters more closely, let's meet Iago, the villain from *Othello*.

Small Group ACTivity

Have a "villain duel." First, get a partner. Each of you chooses to portray one villain (preferably not from the same play). Pick out good phrases and lines, then create a dialogue with them. Perform your villain duel. If you want, you can have your audience vote on which villain "won" the duel. **Scene Suggestions:** Iago and Richard III; Shylock (from *Merchant of Venice)* and Angelo (from *Measure for* Measure). **Variation:** Do the same with a "clown duel." **Scene Suggestions:** Touchstone (from *As You Like It)* and Sir Toby Belch (from *Twelfth Night);* Dogberry (from *Much Ado About Nothing*) and Elbow (from *Measure for Measure).*

Iago

One of the first things you'll notice about Iago is that he is not a subtle man. The very first thing he talks about in Act I, Scene i is how angry he is that Othello has chosen Cassio and not Iago to be his lieutenant. Iago believes that he was better qualified for the promotion and now feels passed over. So already we know that Iago hates Othello for giving the promotion, hates Cassio for getting the promotion, and only plans to stay in Othello's service so that he can get revenge on him. He wastes no time. He immediately goes to Desdemona's father to tell him she has eloped with Othello.

Iago is definitely two-faced. Othello seems to like him and does not suspect that Iago is so angry and evil, so of course Iago decides to use this to his advantage. Iago is also a very jealous person. In a soliloquy at the end of Act I, Scene iii, he mentions that there is a rumor going around that Othello has slept with Iago's wife, Emilia. Iago doesn't know whether this is true or not, but he doesn't seem to be interested in giving either of them the benefit of the doubt. It is then that he begins plotting a way to get back at both Cassio and Othello. He is extremely calculating and calm about it. He decides to suggest to Othello that Desdemona might be in love with Cassio.

Iago has absolutely no scruples about who he has to use to get what he wants. He brings his "friend" (if that word can be used in reference to Iago) Roderigo into it by convincing him that Desdemona is in love with Cassio. This way, Iago knows Roderigo will help him get Cassio dismissed from his station as Othello's lieutenant. Iago is a classic example of the Shakespearean villain: he doesn't care whom he has to hurt in order to get what he wants.

He is also incredibly manipulative. When observing Iago's amazing powers of persuasion, it is easy to wonder what it would be like if Iago were good. With that brilliant mind, that passion for a cause, that ability to plan and to anticipate people's reactions, Iago could do a lot of good! But instead he uses all of those qualities for evil, such as in Act III, Scene iii, when he suggests to Othello that he knows something about Desdemona and Cassio's relationship. Instead of just telling Othello outright, which may make it seem more like the lie it is, Iago instead makes Othello drag it out of him, as if he is reluctant to tell Othello anything that would upset him or ruin his wife's good name. He then has the nerve to warn Othello not to be jealous. All of this, of course, has the effect of reverse psychology: tell Othello his wife's not cheating on him, and he'll believe his wife is cheating on him; tell him not to be jealous, and he'll be jealous. Iago plays him like a fiddle.

As a result, Iago accomplishes his goal—to become Othello's lieutenant—by Act III, Scene iii, only halfway through the play. He spends the rest of the play wreaking his revenge.

We know that Shakespeare's villains are all driven to horrible deeds because of a single, driving goal. It seemed at first that Iago's main goal was to be promoted to the lieutenancy. But once he gets that, he continues to lie to, manipulate, and hurt people. Why? Because his goal wasn't promotion; it was revenge. And revenge is a pretty vague concept: How do you know when you've achieved it? In other words, when do you stop? In Iago's case, we will never quite know, because he is stopped against his will after the other characters finally find out about the awful things he's been doing.

And does Iago ever end up with a psychological punishment? Does he become inflicted with any of Lady Macbeth's madness or Richard III's ghosts? It doesn't seem as if he has a weakness at all, unless it is simply an inability to stop. It is as if he will never be happy.

Describing Iago

There is certainly no shortage of words to describe Iago—even his fellow characters have a few choice ones in Act V, Scene ii, including *wretch, demi-devil, viper, villain*, and *slave*. But here is a list of adjectives and verbs that also describe Iago and his actions:

Adjectives

Two-faced
Jealous
Inadequate
Calculating
Insecure
Unscrupulous
Conniving
Manipulative
Ambitious

Verbs

To get even (with Othello and Cassio)
To hurt (Othello and Cassio)
To convince
To push (Othello to fire Cassio)
To use (Roderigo and Emilio for his plan)
To beat (all of the competition)

Playing Iago

Iago is a wonderful role to play. If you want to start studying the role, listed below are a few scenes and monologues you can look at.

Act I, Scene iii, lines 343–425: two men (Iago and Roderigo)

Act I, Scene iii, lines 426–447: soliloquy (Iago to audience)

Act II, Scene i, lines 234–334: two men (Iago and Roderigo)

Act II, Scene iii, lines 49–66: soliloquy (Iago to audience)

Act II, Scene iii, lines 278–355: two men (Iago and Cassio)

Act II, Scene iii, lines 356–382: soliloquy (Iago to audience)

Act III, Scene iii, lines 103–298: two men (Iago and Othello)

Act III, Scene iii, lines 344–377: one man and one woman (Iago and Emilia)

Act IV, Scene ii, lines 202–277: two men (Iago and Roderigo)

Evil Catch Phrases and Insults

Villains and bad guys often get some really great lines. Here are some from various plays and characters we have already studied that might be memorable:

Othello

[He] will as tenderly be led by the nose as asses are. (Act I, Scene iii, lines 382–384)

[Thou art] as full of quarrel and offence as my young mistress' dog. (Act II, Scene iii, lines 46–47)

Dost thou prate, rogue? (Act II, Scene iii, line 143)

Are his wits safe? Is he not light of brain? (Act IV, Scene i, line 265)

May his pernicious soul rot half a grain a day! (Act V, Scene ii, lines 156–157)

Hamlet

Frailty, thy name is woman. (Act I, Scene ii, line 146)

[You] vicious mole of nature! (Act I, Scene iv, line 24)

[You're] a dull and muddy-mettled rascal. (Act II, Scene ii, line 562)

[You are] pigeon-liver'd and lack gall. (Act II, Scene ii, line 573)

'Tis a vice to know him. (Act V, Scene ii, lines 85–86)

Richard III

Thou lump of foul deformity! (Act I, Scene ii, line 57)

Out of my sight! Thou dost infect my eyes. (Act I, Scene ii, line 152)

Dispute not with her; she is a lunatic. (Act I, Scene iii, line 254)

[You are] deep, hollow, treacherous, and full of guile. (Act II, Scene i, line 38)

The world—'Tis full of thy foul wrongs. (Act IV, Scene iv, line 374)

Romeo and Juliet

Thou wilt fall backward when thou hast more wit. (Act I, Scene iii, line 42)

She speaks, yet she says nothing. (Act II, Scene ii, line 12)

She, good soul, had as lief see a toad, a very toad, as see him. (Act II, Scene iv, lines 198–199)

You rat-catcher! (Act III, Scene i, line 74)

What a pestilent knave is this same. (Act IV, Scene v, line 139)

FOOLS AND CLOWNS

The category of fools and clowns is a pretty broad one, as many of Shakespeare's characters potentially fall into it. A fool isn't necessarily a stupid person; it is more like a court jester. But the term "jester" is misleading, too, as it's not necessarily a little guy with bells on his hat. Similarly, a clown isn't a guy with a big red nose and a rainbow wig. The categories are a little more subtle than that.

Fools, for instance, are usually people employed by a royal court to provide entertainment. Imagine if a stand-up comic like Chris Rock or Jamie Kennedy lived at the White House and performed at the whim of the President: It's a similar concept. Feste in *Twelfth Night* does a lot of singing, King Lear's fool makes jokes, and Touchstone in *As You Like It* is always ready with a sarcastic line or two. A fool's humor tends to be cerebral: the jokes are often about current events or puns; in other words, you sometimes have to know what's going on in the scene to find them funny.

Clowns, on the other hand, are usually ordinary people who end up blundering into humorous situations. Falstaff may be the most famous example of this. Falstaff is actually a knight; comedy is not his chosen career path, and yet that's what he's best known for. Another characteristic of clowns is that there is often a physical side to their humor. They are often awkward, fat, drunk, or all three.

Fools and clowns do have some things in common, the biggest of which is that they provide comic relief. They almost always have something clever or silly to say or do, or are ready with a song to sing. But fools and clowns aren't there just to make us laugh. They often serve important functions. Puck in *A Midsummer Night's Dream* serves as Oberon's messenger and errand boy; Touchstone in *As You Like It* goes into the forest with Rosalind and Celia to provide protection and companionship; Dogberry in *Much Ado About Nothing* is captain of the watch.

There is not necessarily only one fool or clown per play. For instance, *Twelfth Night* has Feste, who is the official court jester; but Sir Toby Belch is definitely a clown (how could he not be a clown, with a name like "Toby Belch"?). *A Midsummer Night's Dream* sports quite a few silly characters: Puck is the obvious choice, but the rude mechanicals are definitely all clowns; what's more, they serve the purpose of entertaining at court (although the play they put on, "Pyramus and Thisbe," is pretty bad entertainment). In this case, the word "rude" doesn't mean impolite; it means unpolished or uneducated—and these guys definitely fit the bill.

To look at a clown in more detail, let's see what we can find out about Bottom from *A Midsummer Night's Dream.*

Bottom

We first meet Bottom, the weaver, in Act I Scene ii, at the first rehearsal for a play. His friend Peter Quince, the carpenter, is the playwright and director, but Bottom seems to have very specific ideas about how the rehearsal is run and what parts people should play, and is therefore forever interrupting and correcting Quince. His ideas are amusingly impractical, as he asks to be allowed to play all three major roles because he thinks he can play them better than anyone else. The idea of Bottom hopping about onstage, asking himself a question, then answering himself as a different character, makes for a pretty funny mental picture. Already we see in him the physical comedy of the true Shakespearean clown.

Bottom and his friends always speak in prose. This is Shakespeare's way of showing us that they're not terribly intelligent. Not only that, but Bottom has a funny way of misusing words while trying to sound smarter than he is. For instance, at the end of the scene, he says, "We will meet, and there we will rehearse most obscenely and courageously" (Act I, Scene ii, lines 103–104). Now, he probably doesn't mean the rehearsal will be *obscene* (which means *disgusting*); he might mean instead that the rehearsal will be *seemly*, which in Shakespeare's time meant *showy* or *sophisticated*.

When we see Bottom again in Act III, Scene i, he and his friends are in the woods rehearsing, with Bottom giving more of his silly suggestions. After watching the rehearsal for a while, Puck changes Bottom's head to that of a donkey. It suddenly becomes clear to us why Shakespeare named the character Bottom: The whole thing was just a big setup for a pun. As you know, another word for *bottom* (as in, rear end) is *ass*, which is also another word for *donkey*. So now that Bottom is a donkey, he is truly an ass.

Bottom is definitely a show-off, and thinks he is smarter and more cultured than he is. He is definitely not a good actor, and yet he thinks he is; he is not handsome (especially with the head of a donkey), and yet he is perfectly willing to believe that the queen of the fairies could fall in love with him. And yet, he is very lovable—once Titania falls in love with Bottom (because of Puck) and showers him with compliments, Bottom bashfully deflects every one. Even Bottom's friends, when he returns to them as himself again, are overjoyed to see him, believing they could not have replaced him in the play.

So Bottom is a true Shakespearean clown. He is just a regular weaver who ends up being dragged into a ridiculous situation. He provides us with physical humor and a certain amount of verbal humor as well.

Describing Bottom

Let's see what words we can come up with for Bottom:

Adjectives	Verbs
Unsophisticated	To act
Impractical	To shine
Silly	To direct
Unrefined	To show-off
Simple	To enjoy (the attentions of the fairies)
Sincere	
Honest	To impress (Theseus and Hippolyta)

Playing Bottom

If you are interested in further study of the role of Bottom, here are some scenes to consider:

Act I, Scene ii: six men (the rude mechanicals)

Act III, Scene i, lines 122–end: one man, one woman, four men or women (Bottom, Titania, and fairies)

Act IV, Scene i, lines 210–end: soliloquy (Bottom to audience)

Act IV, Scene ii: six men (the rude mechanicals)

Act V, Scene i, lines 306–322: monologue (Bottom playing Pyramus to "audience")

111

Large Group ACTivity

Host your own Shakespeare Awards Show. Come up with your own categories, such as "Meanest Villain," "Strongest Woman," "Most Loyal Sidekick," and "Best Speech in Iambic Pentameter." Make it as simple or complex as you like. Let everyone vote on his or her favorite Shakespearean character in each category, then announce the winners. Or if you like, you can make award statues, have people dress up as the characters to accept the awards, and even give acceptance speeches in iambic pentameter or blank verse.

❧ CHAPTER FIVE ❧

GREAT MOMENTS: SHAKESPEARE'S DILEMMAS, HOAXES, AND ROMANCES

 If this were played upon a stage now, I could condemn it as an improbable fiction.

—*Twelfth Night*, ACT III, SCENE IV, LINES 136–137

When it comes right down to it, there is one thing that everybody can appreciate about Shakespeare: We can still relate to him. The things he wrote about are things that still happen to us today: People still fall in love with people their parents hate; they still contemplate suicide; they still play silly tricks on each other.

The joy is that just about everybody can find a Shakespearean character they can relate to. At some point, you'll be sitting out in the audience watching a play that was written ages and ages before you were born, and you might suddenly realize that Shakespeare must have known you, because there you are, up on stage in one of his plays. But whether you see yourself in any of his characters or not, you can't deny that Shakespeare has a timelessness rarely found in other dramatic literature.

And whether or not they withstand the test of time, the fact is that Shakespeare's greatest dramatic moments are very memorable. In just about any social setting, if you mention the words "To be or not to be," the people you're with will recognize them, even if they don't know exactly where they came from. Why? Because that is one of the most memorable moments in all of dramatic literature. And everybody knows who Romeo and Juliet are, even if they can't tell you who wrote the play or exactly how it ends. Why? Because

113

Romeo and Juliet's story has made an impression on all kinds of people throughout the ages. They are so memorable that they transcend social and economic status, not to mention time.

Let's look at a few of Shakespeare's greatest and most memorable moments, then discuss how we can relate to them today.

DILEMMAS

People handle dilemmas in different ways. Some people make lists of pros and cons, and whatever option gets the most pros is the one they go with. Some people don't think about it at all, but go with their instinct—that gut feeling you get that tells you right away which is the safest way to go. Some people talk to a trusted friend, while others poll a bunch of friends and acquaintances: "If you were in my situation, what would you do?" Some people write in a journal. And some people just get paralyzed by the idea of making a decision and don't do anything at all.

It's that last type of dilemma that Shakespeare deals with the most. Again, we're seeing his tendency to put human beings under the microscope: to put a character in a dilemma and see how he or she behaves. It's like reality TV, only we never see a camera crew because there isn't one. These characters are in it for real.

Hamlet

The most famous of all of Shakespeare's dilemmas is found in Hamlet's "to be or not to be" speech. At that moment, Hamlet is actually contemplating suicide. He can't decide whether he would rather live or take his chances with death.

Hamlet's way of dealing with this dilemma is to talk it through out loud—kind of a verbal pro and con list. First, he wonders if it is noble to simply suffer through all the problems of life, or whether it would be nobler to stand up to those problems by ending them once and for all (i.e., by killing himself):

> *Whether 'tis nobler in the mind to suffer*
> *The slings and arrows of outrageous fortune,*
> *Or to take arms against a sea of troubles,*
> *And by opposing end them?*
>
> (Act III, Scene i, lines 57–60)

He compares death to sleep, and speaks about how great it would be just to go to sleep forever and get away from his problems; but then he worries about what dreams he could have while sleeping the sleep of death. They could very well be nightmares:

> *To die, to sleep;*
> *To sleep, perchance to dream: ay, there's the rub;*
> *For in that sleep of death what dreams may come*
> *When we have shuffled off this mortal coil,*
> *Must give us pause.*
>
> (Act III, Scene i, Lines 64–68)

But if suicide were the best way to end one's problems, Hamlet wonders, wouldn't everyone be doing it? The problem is that no one has ever come back from death to tell us what it's like; it could very well be worse than life:

> *For who would bear the whips and scorns of time,*
> *…When he himself might quietus make*
> *With a bare bodkin?*
>
> (Act III, Scene i, lines 70, 75–76)

So instead we bear the problems of life, concludes Hamlet, rather than facing the unknown and possibly worse problems of death. And as a result, we choose to do nothing:

> *Thus conscience doth make cowards of us all;*
> *…And enterprises of great pitch and moment*
> *With this regard their currents turn awry,*
> *And lose the name of action.*
>
> (Act III, Scene i, Lines 83, 86–88)

Interestingly, modern knowledge of psychology casts a new light on this soliloquy. Any psychologist could tell you that Hamlet is depressed. He shows so many of the symptoms: He is often sad, sometimes without reason; the things and people that he liked no longer bring him happiness; he is lethargic and indecisive; he seems to have difficulty concentrating, and he contemplates suicide.

The odd thing is that—like a truly depressed person—Hamlet doesn't seem to realize he has more than just two options open to him. The way he sees it, he can live and just silently suffer through all the awful things life is throwing at him, or he can die and take his chances. But there is a third option that he doesn't consider in this speech: He can choose life and *action*. He can, if he tries, solve his father's murder, patch things up with Ophelia and his mother, and bring Claudius to justice. And to his credit, he does eventually do some of these things, and who knows how many more he would have accomplished if Claudius had not plotted his death in the swordfight against Laertes. But it is interesting to wonder what would have happened if Hamlet had taken that third option and immediately followed it through to the end. How would the end of *Hamlet* be different?

Small Group ACTivity

Write your own ending. Choose a great moment from any Shakespeare play and imagine what would have happened if that moment ended in a completely different way. Re-write the scene using your new ending and perform it for an audience. Then, perform the same scene in its original form. Ask the audience to compare the two. Which is better, and why? How would the changed scene affect the rest of the play?

King Lear

Imagine yourself in the following scenario: You have something really valuable to give away, such as a house, a collection of brand-name clothes, a really nice stereo, or some exquisite jewelry. Now imagine that there are three people you could give it to...say, your three best friends. Secretly, you love one of them more than the other two, but you would never say that, even though you're pretty sure you're going to give the valuables to that person.

What's the dilemma? You have to decide which of them to give your valuables to, or whether to divide them among all three of them. How do you decide? You hold a party, and during the party you ask each of the three to publicly say how much they love you (okay, so you're a fairly conceited person). Based on their speeches, you will decide which of them gets what. So the first two go on and on about how great you are and how incredibly much they love you, more than any other human being, and it really feels pretty good. But you're waiting for the third one, your favorite. But when it's her turn, she's very quiet and says she has nothing to say. You can't believe it. She's supposed to be the one that loves you the most, she's the one you were going to give everything to—the whole stereo, all the jewelry, whatever—and here she is saying she has nothing to say! What do you do?

If you were Shakespeare's King Lear, you'd banish her from your kingdom and divide it between the other two daughters. But the plan pretty much backfires from the start, because the other two were only saying such nice things because they wanted the land. So when Lear tries to stay with them, they kick him out.

As a teenager, you probably won't have to deal with an issue like this for a long, long time, but people are going through it every day. As they get older, they have to decide when they should stop trying to take care of themselves, and have someone do it for them. And if someone else takes care of them, who should that person be? Sometimes the very people they would expect to depend on in their old age—their children or grandchildren—are the ones who abandon them.

In *King Lear*, Shakespeare deals with a lot of issues we still deal with today, such as the concept of family ties. Do you have to love someone just because you're related to them? Are you obligated to take care of someone after they give you a really nice gift? How far does loyalty really reach?

Let's take a look at what Cordelia (the third daughter) says to her father, and talk about what we would do if we were in Lear's shoes.

After her sisters finish their flowery, excessive speeches, Lear turns to his youngest daughter and says he's saved the best part of his kingdom for her: "To thee and thine hereditary ever remain this ample third of our fair kingdom" (Act I, Scene i, lines 88–89). He will give it to her if she has something wonderful to say about her love for him: "What can you say to draw a third more opulent than your sisters'? Speak" (Act I, Scene i, lines 94–95). But she has nothing to say, and upon being prodded, explains that what she feels cannot be expressed in words and that she only loves him as much as a daughter is expected to love a father:

> *Unhappy that I am, I cannot heave*
> *My heart into my mouth. I love your Majesty*
> *According to my bond, no more nor less.*
> (Act I, Scene i, lines 100–103)

She points out that it doesn't make sense for her sisters to be married if they actually love their father 100% (as they claim to): "Why have my sisters' husbands if they say they love you all?" (Act I, Scene i, Lines 109–110). Cordelia says that when she gets married, her husband will get half her love, and her father will get the other half:

> *Haply, when I shall wed,*
> *That lord whose hand must take my plight shall carry*
> *Half my love with him, half my care and duty.*
> *Sure I shall never marry like my sisters,*
> *To love my father all.*
> (Act I, Scene i, lines 110–115)

This is not, of course, what her father wants to hear, for several reasons. First, it must be embarrassing for his "favorite" daughter to be telling him this in front of all these important people. Second, he's having to re-think his priorities: He thought he loved Cordelia the most, but what if she doesn't love him the most back? Third, what does he do with the rest of his kingdom?

Unlike Hamlet, Lear makes a snap decision, mostly to save face. He tells her she will get no part of his kingdom (instead, he divides the part he was saving for her between the other two daughters), marries her off to the first person who will take her, and banishes her from his kingdom—all because she wouldn't lie! Of course, he spends the rest of the play dealing with the repercussions of this decision, which turns out to be a bad one.

If you've ever read an interview with someone who has won the lottery, you know that after winning all that money, they suddenly have a lot of friends. Their frequent complaint is that it is now difficult to tell who truly likes them and who only likes them for their money (and again, there have been entire reality TV shows based on this concept). Lear is basically having the same problem. His elder daughters only want the land; and although Cordelia doesn't care about the land at all, the irony is that her honesty makes her lose both the land and her father's love.

Other Great Dilemmas

Measure for Measure
Should Isabella give in to Claudio's demands, or let her brother die?

Twelfth Night
Viola realizes that Olivia is in love with her male disguise. How can she woo Olivia on Orsino's behalf without being the object of her affections?

All's Well that Ends Well
Bertram says he won't come back to Helena unless she completes an impossible task. How can she get him back?

Small Group ACTivity

Did you notice how the dilemmas above sound like modern-day soap opera synopses? Find a synopsis from a current soap opera and use it to write your own dilemma scene from a "new" Shakespeare play. Then, cast and perform the scene. **Variation:** Take a dilemma from a Shakespeare play and put it into modern language, then perform it as if it were a scene from a soap opera.

Small Group ACTivity

Divide up your kingdom. Put yourself in Lear's position and imagine that you have a kingdom to give away and three people to give it to. Then, devise a way to decide how to divide it up. Will it be an essay contest? Will you interview their friends to find out if they deserve it? Will you even tell them what they're competing for, or keep it a secret until the last minute? Write a short outline of your plan, then compare it with others'. Which is the best plan? Try acting them out and see what happens.

HOAXES

Throughout history, human beings have loved playing tricks on each other: It's a pastime we will never tire of. In Elizabethan times, April Fool's Day was not yet a holiday, but that certainly didn't stop people from playing tricks on each other. Fooling some poor soul was always good for a laugh, and if you were mad at someone, it was also a great way to get revenge. Nowadays, there are entire books, websites, and television series based on the concept of practical jokes, not to mention the hoax emails that are constantly circling the Internet, so hoaxes are just as familiar a subject to us as they were to Elizabethans.

Shakespeare was no stranger to hoaxes and included a lot of them in his plays. He was always switching identical twins to fool people, causing characters to fall in love with the wrong guy or girl, and forging silly letters for various purposes.

Let's look at a couple of Shakespeare's most hilarious hoaxes.

Malvolio in *Twelfth Night*

At first, Malvolio seems to be one of those uptight guys who never smiles. He is the Countess Olivia's steward (stewards were in charge of things like overseeing servants and managing financial accounts), and he takes his post *very* seriously. But as it turns out, he's just waiting for the right woman to come along—and that's what ends up making him the butt of a pretty funny joke.

Malvolio is an unpopular guy, because he's always going around abusing his power and acting superior. One night when Toby, Andrew, and the Fool are up partying, Maria comes to warn them that if they don't quiet down, Malvolio will come yell at them, and sure enough, he comes and scolds them all as if they were children. Maria decides she's had quite enough of his obnoxious, holier-than-thou behavior, and that's when the plan for a trick begins.

Maria's handwriting happens to look a lot like Olivia's, and Maria takes advantage of that fact by forging a love letter from Olivia and leaving it where Malvolio will find it, so he'll think Olivia is in love with him.

The result is pretty funny. The letter convinces Malvolio that Olivia wants him to dress up in yellow stockings, smile all the time, and be confrontational with Sir Toby. Thinking that's the best way to win her love, Malvolio starts acting ridiculously, much to the horror and exasperation of Olivia and the hilarity of his four tormentors. Not only is Olivia not in love with Malvolio, but she hates yellow, and is in mourning for her brother, which would make Malvolio's smiling very inappropriate. In fact, he makes such a fool of himself that Olivia thinks he's crazy. Sir Toby takes advantage of this and locks him up.

Of course, once Olivia actually speaks to Malvolio about it and sees the letter, she knows what has happened and sets him straight. But the damage has been done, and Maria and her friends have had their fun. Malvolio is very much embarrassed and vows revenge upon them all…and who knows, perhaps the stage is set for Malvolio to play a practical joke on Maria and her friends.

Whatever happens, we can't help but feel a little sorry for Malvolio. Sure, he's pompous and annoying at the beginning, but it is a pretty nasty (although funny) prank they play on him. The poor guy ends up making an idiot of himself in front of the woman he's in love with, not to mention everybody else. He plays right into their hands.

The funny thing about this practical joke is that it's just like something that would happen today. People behave so strangely when they have crushes on other people; they might not wear yellow hose, but there are certainly a lot of ways to fool someone into thinking someone else likes them. Imagine, Shakespeare was writing about jokes that people still play on each other 400 years later!

Puck in *A Midsummer Night's Dream*

Many cultures have myths or legends about pranksters. The Native Americans have the coyote, who uses his sly wits to survive. The Irish have the leprechaun, and the English have Puck, or Robin Goodfellow. As we discussed in chapter three, Puck is an impish character from English folklore who played pranks on people. In *A Midsummer Night's Dream,* he is no different. Oberon, king of the fairies, takes advantage of Puck's trickster nature to get revenge on his wife Titania, with whom he is having an argument. He tells Puck about a flower whose juice, when applied to a person's eyelids, will make them fall in love with the first person they see when they wake up.

But Puck, of course, can't just leave it at that. He does put the juice on Titania's eyes, as Oberon asks, but then he sees Bottom. As soon as he lays eyes on Bottom, he knows instantly what he wants to do. Puck changes Bottom's head into an ass's head, then makes sure he's near Titania when she wakes up. What a great joke to play on the queen of the fairies, to make her fall in love with a stupid, bumbling, half-man half-donkey!

Needless to say, Puck's pranks can't exactly be recreated in our modern-day world. They mostly involve magic and imaginary potions. But we can certainly identify with the irresistible urge to meddle in others' business, to see what happens when you stir up a situation. And Puck obviously appreciates a good pun. Imagine coming across a man named Bottom: It must have been irresistible! How could he stop himself from making Bottom into an ass?

Of course, everything gets put right in the end (except Bottom still makes a fool of himself, but he was that way to begin with). When it all comes down to it, Puck's tricks don't cause any real harm. But it's clear that there's nothing he enjoys like a good laugh at someone else's expense.

Shakespeare can imagine all kinds of hoaxes, from simple ones that could easily be recreated (like forged love letters) to fantastical, magical ones (like love potion). For the most part, though, Shakespeare's practical jokes don't hurt anybody, turn out all right in the end, and make for fun entertainment in between. One thing that hasn't changed in 400 years is that we all like to have a good laugh!

Other Great Hoaxes

Much Ado about Nothing

The evil Don John and his buddies make Claudio think that his fiancée, Hero, is cheating on him.

The Merry Wives of Windsor

Mistress Ford and Mistress Page find out Falstaff is wooing them both, and punish him for it by leading him out in the woods where their friends attack him.

As You Like It

Rosalind (disguised as Ganymede) gets Phoebe to agree to marry Silvius if Ganymede turns out to be a woman.

Small Group ACTivity

Have you noticed that the hoaxes above read like sitcom plots? Take any plot from a current sitcom and write a Shakespeare-style scene based on it. Then, perform it with the other members of your group. **Variation:** Take any Shakespearean hoax and make it into a scene from a sitcom using modern language.

ROMANCES

There are probably just about as many different ways of falling in love as there are couples. The spectrum ranges from arranged marriages to love at first sight. Somehow, Shakespeare managed to show us a lot of the places along that spectrum, with a lot of different ways of showing love. There is Lady Macbeth, whose love for her husband is tied up with her ambition for him, and who shows that love by pushing him to the limits of his abilities as a leader and a criminal. And in contrast, there is Titania, who loves Bottom the second she sees him, ass-head and all (albeit, as we have just discussed, with the help of some magic), and who expresses her love by ordering the fairies in her command to attend to Bottom's every whim.

In some cases, the love story is the central plot of a Shakespeare play, as in *Romeo and Juliet* and *Much Ado About Nothing*. And in other cases, it is present, but not necessarily the central feature, as in *Hamlet* or *Macbeth*. But considering that the subject of romance appears in nearly every single one of Shakespeare's plays, it's clear that love is a subject that has held the attention of the human psyche for centuries. Most of the plots of today's television shows and movies somehow involve love or dating or marriage in some way. Again, Shakespeare proves that, even though 400 years have gone by, we really haven't changed all that much as human beings.

When it comes right down to it, the subject of love frequently has us on the edge of our seats. "Will he kiss her?" we wonder, or, "Will she reject him?" And Shakespeare frequently raises the stakes. In his world, a boy will die for the love of a girl he's met only days ago, and a woman will marry a man just because he picks the right casket. When it comes to love, Shakespeare means business. It isn't kids going on a date to the movies; it's people fighting battles or drinking poison or leaving their families or their religions for the one they love.

Romeo and Juliet

We can't talk about great romances in Shakespeare without mentioning Romeo and Juliet. In fact, you can't really talk about great romances in general without mentioning them. Their love story has captured the world's imagination for centuries, and it's easy to see why: It's dramatic, heartbreaking, violent, epic, and oh-so-romantic. It has a little something for everyone, from swordfights and dramatic deaths to kissing and…well, more dramatic deaths.

As we discovered in chapter four, Romeo is a romantic guy to start with. He's always falling head over heels in love with someone. This time it just happens to be the daughter of his family's sworn enemy, which might even make it a little more exciting.

But Juliet is just as taken with Romeo, even though her mother and father have arranged for her to marry a man named Paris. And even though she is not quite 14 years old, her mother thinks it is high time she was married.

In the classic tradition of love at first sight, those obstacles—warring families, pre-arranged suitors—fall away when Romeo and Juliet first meet. It's a classic flirtation, full of metaphors. For instance, Romeo never comes out and says he wants to kiss Juliet; it's much more fun to compare her to a shrine and himself to a pilgrim, and see what she says. And suddenly here is Juliet in the middle of her parents' masquerade ball, kissing some boy she just met who may or may not (for all she knows) be Paris, her husband-to-be.

But as silly as it seems for Romeo and Juliet to know they're destined to be together as soon as they meet, the fact is that that sort of thing does happen in real life. Not often, certainly, but it does happen. Romeo and Juliet's story reminds us that there is no formula for falling in love. Read all the Ann Landers columns and *Seventeen* articles you want on the subject; the fact is that no one can tell you how to find the person you're going to marry, and once you find them, how to hold onto them. Romance comes in all shapes and sizes; you're just as likely to find a couple who married two weeks after they met and stayed married for 50 years as you are to find a couple who knew (and possibly even disliked) each other throughout their entire childhoods before realizing they loved each other. Somehow, Shakespeare realized this important feature of human romance and brought it out in his plays. And as a result, we have Romeo and Juliet meeting, falling in love, marrying, and dying within a matter of days, and it has become one of the most famous love stories of all time.

As the story unfolds, we follow Romeo and Juliet through clandestine meetings, messages exchanged through Juliet's nurse, their secret wedding, the killing of Tybalt and Mercutio, the procurement of sleeping potions, and the couple's unfortunate demise. But the story isn't just about the tragic love between two teenagers. Shakespeare is also making the case that love serves a higher purpose. The very first thing we find out about Romeo and Juliet is that they're from enemy houses, and this fact continues to be a problem throughout the play. But it is not until Romeo and Juliet die that the families drop their feud. Without ever intending to, the two young lovers have resolved an age-old quarrel, healing wounds that no one ever thought would heal. In fact, Romeo and Juliet have achieved in death something they may never have achieved in life, so in a way, they are the ultimate sacrifice. They have sacrificed themselves for love, to be sure; but it is not only for the passionate, romantic love between the two of them, but for the love that was lacking for so long between their two families. It is definitely a tragedy, but it does remind us of that joyous saying, "Love conquers all."

Large Group ACTivity

What if Shakespeare's lovers appeared on a television talk show to try to work through their problems? Create your own talk show, with some of Shakespeare's famous couples—such as a modern-day Romeo and Juliet or Titania and Bottom—as the featured guests. You'll need to cast the lovers, a host, and some audience members. Remember to pick a theme: "How to say together when your families want to kill each other," or "I love my boyfriend even though he has a donkey's head." Then have the lovers explain the problem, the host ask questions and make comments, and the audience members dispense advice on how to handle star-crossed love or why Titania should kick that donkey out the door.

Benedick and Beatrice

On the other side of the spectrum, there is the love story from *Much Ado About Nothing*. There is nothing tragic about it; in fact, it's quite funny. Actually, Benedick and Beatrice's romance is just about as diametrically opposite of Romeo and Juliet's as you can get.

For starters, they've known each other for a long time, and they hate each other. Well, perhaps "hate" is too strong a word; they are not fond of one another, and are continually getting into battles of wits or talking behind the other's back. In addition, they both swear they will never marry.

Once they dance together at a masked ball, their dislike for one another becomes much stronger. Benedick recognizes Beatrice, but she does not recognize him, and says such horrible things to him about Benedick (thinking he is someone else) that Benedick is shocked. He says later that he could hardly keep up his disguise.

So how does this end up being a great romance? Their friends decide to set them up. After all, who doesn't like a good challenge now and then? Knowing Benedick is by himself in the garden, they have a conversation they allow him to "overhear" about how much Beatrice loves him, but it's a shame because Benedick says he'll never marry. Then, they do the same for Beatrice. Once the seeds are planted, Beatrice and Benedick's affection for one another grows quickly, and eventually they participate in the wedding at the end of the play doing what they each said they never would: getting married.

It's almost as if Shakespeare is telling us that sometimes we don't know what's best for us. Benedick and Beatrice didn't know what fate had in store for them, but somehow their friends saw it for them and led them in the right direction, toward each other. That's the great thing about friends—sometimes they know us better than we know ourselves.

The line between love and hate can sometimes be very fine, because they are both very passionate emotions and Benedick and Beatrice are passionate people. They have just found a way to cross the line together.

Other Great Romances

A Midsummer Night's Dream
Titania and Bottom, with the help of some of Puck's love potion.

Hamlet
Hamlet and Ophelia–those most have been some amazing love letters!

King Lear
Cordelia and the King of France, who marries her even though she has no land and no money.

Small Group ACTivity

Choose a modern-day dilemma, hoax, or romance. It can be something you have experienced in your own life, something from TV, the Internet, the news, or something you make up entirely. Then, write a scene from a "Shakespeare" play based on it. Perform the scene for an audience and ask them what they think.

Section Three

PERFORMING SHAKESPEARE: ACTORS AND AUDIENCES

ACTING SHAKESPEARE

All the world's a stage
And all the men and women merely
players.
—*As You Like It*, ACT II, SCENE VII, LINES 146–147

THE PROBLEM OF ACTING

The strange thing about acting is that there is not one "right" way to do it. It doesn't matter whether you're acting in a Shakespeare play or in the latest Jackie Chan movie; the fact is that people will always have differing opinions about what makes good acting.

For instance, you might think Keanu Reeves is an absolute genius when it comes to portraying his roles, while your best friend might be convinced that Reeves is little more than a chimpanzee with a script. But the problem of figuring out what makes good acting is not a new one. Even folks in Shakespeare's time had favorite actors, and actors they thought weren't very good at all.

One reason for this is "the human factor"—people are completely different from one another in real life. Think about it: The way you behave when you're angry may be completely different from the way one of your classmates behaves when angry. Perhaps you get red in the face and start yelling, while your classmate grows pale and quiet. So if you see an actor playing a character who is angry and he isn't red-faced and yelling, you might have trouble

SUBJECTIVE

When reality or truth is perceived by an individual and their opinion, as opposed to being a universal truth that everyone agrees upon. Acting is a subjective art, meaning that just because one person perceives it to be good does not make that a universal truth.

believing his performance. And that's just the tip of the iceberg of reasons that acting is such a *subjective* craft.

While there is just one right answer to the question, "What is two plus two?", there might be hundreds of right answers to the question, "What is the most convincing way to play King Richard III?" This makes acting pretty difficult to teach, as well. After all, there are all kinds of convincing ways to play Shakespeare's evil king, but all of them are pretty tough to explain. But even if, just for the sake of argument, I could tell you all the right things to do to portray Richard III (which I can't), you could still have an off day or forget part of your costume or misunderstand something I said, and your audience might go away thinking, "I just don't believe he's an evil king."

TECHNIQUE

Any method of acting.

All of this is a roundabout way of saying that different actors have different *techniques*, or concepts a person uses to become a good actor. In fact, there are as many different ways of acting as there are actors. But certain acting techniques have characteristics in common, and techniques have changed over the years, just like clothing styles and language.

In this chapter, we'll look at various acting techniques from Shakespeare's time until now. We'll also talk about how to act Shakespeare and discuss some steps you can use if you ever have to perform a scene.

Small Group ACTivity

What is the purpose of acting? Write down a list of all the reasons you think people act. Is it to entertain? Is it to get attention? Is it to express a specific viewpoint or to move the audience to action? What other reasons can you think of? Discuss your list with your group. Additionally, if you plan to become a professional actor when you grow up, think about and discuss the reasons behind your own specific career goals.

ACTING TECHNIQUES: ART VERSUS LIFE

Some people in Shakespeare's time believed that acting was, as Hamlet says, "holding a mirror up to nature." You might have heard that phrase's modern equivalent, "art reflects life." What these phrases mean is that it is the actor's job to show what real life is like, so that, as an audience member, you could watch that actor's performance and say to yourself, "Yes, that is exactly what that situation is like in real life."

The problem is that people's idea of what is *realistic* has changed over the years. The easiest way to understand this is to think in terms of painting versus photography. Before cameras existed, the only way you could get a picture of a face (or anything else, for that matter) was by drawing or painting a portrait of it. But painters can make subjective interpretations of their subjects through such techniques as impressionism or cubism. They can change a person's features as they paint—make brown eyes blue, or take out the grey in the hair, or accidentally make the nose smaller than it is. If you had never seen a photograph, you might look at that portrait and say, "It looks just like her!" Now, however, we think of photographs as being much more accurate or "true to life" than paintings.

REALISTIC

A style of acting that strives to be more believable and natural and less dramatic, artificial, and overdone.

Small Group ACTivity

Make a list of your favorite actors. They can be actors from movies, television, the stage, or any combination. If you want, you can list the role or roles in which each actor on your list showed his or her best attributes or did his or her best work. Take a few moments to look at the list and think about what all the actors on your list have in common. In your opinion, what makes a good actor? Then, make a list of attributes you think are important for good acting. When you are finished, compare your list with the other people in your group. Do certain names appear on some or all of the actor lists? Did you list any of the same characteristics of good acting on your attributes list? Discuss why each of you chose the actors and attributes you did. If you disagree, discuss the reasons why.

So it is with acting. If we could watch an Elizabethan actor today, we might think that his acting is over the top and not believable at all, whereas if he saw one of our actors, he might think the acting was lacking in emotion or depth. Both actors might call their styles "realistic"—it's just that their definitions of realistic are different from each other.

Elizabethan Acting

When it comes right down to it, we don't really know what acting style the actors of Shakespeare's time used. We can find clues in the way the productions were put on and in the writings of the time, but short of having the original performances on video, we really can't know what the acting style was like.

Shakespeare's Advice for Actors

Most of the clues Shakespeare himself gives us are in Hamlet's famous speech to the players in Act III, Scene ii. A traveling theater troupe has come to visit Prince Hamlet's castle, and Hamlet takes some time with the actors to tell them how to put on their best performance:

1. He tells them to make sure they speak smoothly and clearly, but that he hates it when actors overenunciate: "Speak the speech…trippingly on the tongue; but if you mouth it, as many of our players do, I had as lief the town-crier spoke my lines."

2. He then warns against making jerky, exaggerated hand motions, but instead suggests the actors make their body movements controlled and natural, even when there is great emotion in the lines they are speaking: "Nor do not saw the air too much with your hand, thus, but use all gently; for in the very torrent, tempest, and, as I may say, whirlwind of your passion, you must acquire and beget a temperance that may give it a smoothness."

3. Next, he tells how annoying it is to see player overact. He can't stand it when actors just get on stage and shout, or are overly emotional: "O, it offends me to the soul to hear a robustious, periwig-pated fellow tear a passion to tatters, to very rags."

4. He then warns against the opposite problem, that is, being too quiet and therefore boring; he reminds them that the whole point of acting is to show the world as it really is and to imitate human life accurately: "Be not too tame neither, but let your own discretion be your tutor. …anything so o'erdone is from the purpose of playing, whose end…is to hold…the mirror up to nature…O, there be players that I have seen play and heard others praise…that…have so strutted and bellowed…they imitated humanity so abominably."

You can read *Hamlet* Act III, Scene ii yourself for the entire text of Hamlet's advice to the players. If we assume that Shakespeare is using the character Hamlet to show his own true feelings about good acting technique, then it is clear that it was very important to Shakespeare to portray human life as accurately as possible.

Spontaneity

Regardless of how Elizabethan actors chose to portray their roles, they certainly didn't have much time to practice. Research shows that Elizabethan theatre companies could put a play together in as little as one day. That's right, *one day* of rehearsal. If you were an actor in Shakespeare's time, you would be given your side, memorize your lines the night before, go to the theatre in the morning to learn where your character entered and exited the stage and to be given your costume, and then the play started at about two o'clock in the afternoon. After the play was over, you would either start learning a new play for the next day or relearn the lines to a play that you might have done six months ago. The average Elizabethan theatre company usually had anywhere from 20 to 40 plays in their *repertoire*—in other words, there were 20 to 40 plays that they knew and could put on at any time. Since they performed six days a week all year long, they had to make sure their audiences didn't get bored and go somewhere else for their entertainment, so they put on a different play every day.

> **REPERTOIRE**
>
> A number of plays that a single theatre company is able to perform at any time.

In comparison, theatre companies today take as long as ten weeks to rehearse their plays. So getting a play ready for an audience in a single day is pretty hard for us to imagine. On the other hand, such a fast schedule totally eliminates the problem of trying to make a play look natural and spontaneous. These days, much of the rehearsal process is spent trying to make it seem like everything on stage is happening for the first time; actors and directors alike are concerned with making sure the play doesn't seem "too rehearsed." But in Shakespeare's time, with their one-day rehearsals, performances probably never looked too rehearsed because they simply weren't. The spontaneity didn't have to be manufactured because it was there already.

No Women Allowed

Another important aspect of acting in Shakespeare's time is that it was all done by men. Women were not allowed to be actors, so all the female roles were played by young men or boys. (This was the reason why Gwyneth Paltrow's character in the film *Shakespeare in Love* had to pretend to be a boy in order to perform in Shakespeare's play.) Boys playing women and girls was a *convention* that was wholeheartedly accepted by the Elizabethan audience. In other words, you would never hear an audience member complain, "I don't believe that's Juliet up there. You can tell that's really a boy playing her. Why don't they get a girl to play her instead?" Of course audiences knew those were boys up there playing women, but it wasn't something that bothered them, because that was just the way things were. There are two ways to look at this:

CONVENTION

Any established theatrical practice that the audience buys into.

1. Either the boys were such good actors that they could play women just as well as women could (which is highly unlikely!), or...

2. They acted nothing like real women, but nobody cared because it simply wasn't socially acceptable to let real women put themselves on display.

Classroom ACTivity

Choose a scene that has both male and female characters in it, and then try acting it out using all boys or all girls. Then do the same scene with the proper genders playing the proper roles. How does it affect the scene? **Scene Suggestions:** *A Midsummer Night's Dream,* Act III, Scene ii; *The Merchant of Venice,* Act IV, Scene i. **Variation:** Try an all-male scene using all female actors, or vice versa. Discuss how it affects the scene. **Scene Suggestions:** *Romeo and Juliet,* Act I, Scene iii; *The Tempest,* Act II, Scene i.

Later Acting Techniques

More recently—in the past 100 years or so—Shakespearean acting technique became more stylized and dramatic. There was the feeling that Shakespeare was very important and elevated, and therefore unworthy of casual, conversational interpretation.

Silent Films

The earliest surviving films of Shakespeare performances are silent films. At the turn of the 20th century, it was impossible to make a film with sound, so what you would see was a moving picture with the occasional screen of text scattered in between to tell you what was going on. The acting technique of these early, silent Shakespeare films—most of which were made between 1899 and 1920—is extremely stylized. Everything had to be shown through movement, so the gestures were exaggerated. Watching these silent films, you almost feel as if you are watching theatre for children. It is very simplified and mechanical. Any emotion is shown through movement. The movements are either very large or are done repeatedly. A character who wants you to know that he is laughing might hold his sides and shake, then slap his knee two or three times. For sadness, he covers his face with both hands and shakes his shoulders. For love, he kneels, holds his hands to his heart for several seconds, and looks adoringly at his beloved...you get the idea.

It seems that very little thought underlies the action in this style of acting. That is, there is only mechanical motion to represent what the character is thinking and feeling. Imagine, for instance, having to perform a Shakespeare scene where you have to tell someone you love him or her. If you expressed it only physically, as in the acting style of the early 20th century, you might be thinking, "If I bring my hands to my heart and look adoringly, the audience will think I love this person." But if you were acting realistically, you would more likely be thinking, "I really love this person," and your body would simply do whatever came along with that.

Modern Acting Techniques

Since the time that Shakespeare wrote his famous plays, we have learned much about the human mind and how it works. This discipline, as you know, is called psychology—and it may surprise you to learn that it did not exist as a formal study in Shakespeare's time. Psychology has a lot of influence on the acting technique of today, thanks in part to the methods developed by the great Russian teacher/director, **Konstantin Stanislavski**. When using a modern acting technique in Shakespeare, however, it is important to remember that the words you are speaking were written in a time when the human mind was considered to be more straightforward than it is today.

STANISLAVSKI, KONSTANTIN (1863–1938)

A Russian actor, director, and teacher, Stanislavski revolutionized acting technique by creating a more simplified yet intensely psychological style of acting. He laid the groundwork for what eventually became Method acting in America. He also founded the Moscow Art Theatre.

Acting and Thinking

Shakespeare's characters think out loud. They are very frank. True, some of them are liars, but even they share their true feelings, if only in a soliloquy to the audience (when they think they're alone). For the most part, they say what they mean and mean what they say. The things that come out of their mouths are not planned in advance; rather, they speak the thoughts that occur to them *at that very moment*. Shakespeare's characters live very much "in the now."

The great introspective, dramatic pauses of modern acting have no place in Shakespeare. Indeed, if you were to fall silent to "think" in the middle of a speech, it would interrupt the rhythm of the verse. But rhythm or no, taking such a pause would simply not be accurate, because Shakespeare's characters think and speak at the same time, and therefore have no need for big pauses.

Acting and Emotion

The same can be said for emotions. The emotion is right there in Shakespeare's words, not worked up between the lines. If extreme emotions are necessary—which they very often are in Shakespeare—you must trust that he will give you the words necessary to get that emotion across to the audience. There is no need to manufacture them. Instead, as you speak Shakespeare's language, *feel* it. Let the words roll around on your tongue, and pay attention to the thoughts and feelings those words evoke. Much of Shakespeare's language is *visceral* and *onomatopoetic*—he chooses words because they sound like what they mean, or evoke certain feelings. So trust that. Emotionally speaking, Shakespeare's language will lead you where you need to go.

A director once said "Your first obligation is to tell the story." And you know what? He is right! Shakespeare is a master storyteller, and once I trusted that and merely focused on what was going on in the story, the emotion took care of itself. Forget the warm fuzzies; just tell the audience what happened. If you ever feel like you are getting mired down with "looking angry" or "being sad," just think to yourself, "What do I want to do to the other person? What do I want out of this scene?" If you just focus on what your character wants, you'll be fine.

The bottom line: Play goals, not emotions. Shakespeare's characters are busy *doing* things, not *feeling* things—and as an actor, you should be, too.

VISCERAL

Something so compelling as to be felt with the whole body.

ONOMATOPOETIC

When words sound like what they mean, or imitate the sound of the item they describe, such as "boom" or "whoosh." Shakespeare uses a lot of onomatopoeia.

Solo ACTivity

Watch two different productions of the same Shakespeare play and compare the two. Ideally, try and make at least one of them a live production. If both are movies, try to get them from different time periods, such as Laurence Olivier's *Hamlet* (1948) and Ethan Hawke's *Hamlet* (2000) (see Appendix B for a list of Shakespeare on film). Compare the acting styles of the various actors. Which seems more believable to you, and why? What do they have in common? How does the setting of the play (where and when it takes place) affect the acting and the story?

HOW TO ACT SHAKESPEARE: A STEP-BY-STEP APPROACH

There are many different techniques for acting Shakespeare, and most of them are excellent. I can take you through my process and tell you the things I've learned along the way, but for many people, acting is an intensely personal process, and they develop their own ways of doing it. You will, too.

You do not have to carry out all the suggestions that follow; pick and choose those you think you might need. They also don't have to be followed in order, and you can come back and redo any of the exercises should the scene become wooden or stale once you get it on its feet. The goal here is honesty, not perfection.

No British, Please!

As you do your readings, remember that it is not necessary to use any sort of accent. Many people think that using a British accent is a more accurate or proper way to do Shakespeare. Not true! In fact, some experts say that the contemporary American accent is closer to how the Elizabethans sounded than the contemporary British accent. And even if you don't have a standard American accent, you will still feel more relaxed—and therefore have better vocal production—if you use your own accent.

Another excellent reason not to use an English accent: Many of Shakespeare's characters aren't even English! Hamlet is Danish, Macbeth is Scottish, Romeo and Juliet are Italian... you get the idea. If you really want to, you could try doing an accent for your character's nation of origin, but that might simply distract your audience from the story itself, which is what's most important.

A small handful of Shakespeare's characters are supposed to have accents; their peculiar way of speaking is intrinsic to their character. Two notable examples of this come from *The Merry Wives of Windsor*, where Doctor Caius of France and Sir Hugh Evans of Wales are virtually unintelligible to their English companions. In both of their cases, Shakespeare has actually written their lines to reflect their accent. But for the most part, it is wisest just to stick to the way you normally speak.

Small Group ACTivity

Compare accents. If you can do a British accent, try doing a scene or monologue twice through, once using a British accent, once using your own accent. If you can't or don't feel comfortable, compare two filmed or taped versions of the same play, one British, one American. In either case, compare how the accents affect the play and the way the characters are portrayed. Which is easier to do? Which is more convincing to you?

Look and Listen

Many of the exercises that follow require you to make eye contact with your partner and truly listen to what he or she is saying. This is something you should make a habit of in your acting. Because the lines are written out for you on the page, it is easy to let your mind wander. You might think you can get by just by listening for the last word in their line, then saying your own line, and otherwise letting your brain do anything at all—skipping ahead to see how the scene ends, thinking about what you'll do after school, making mental a list of all the homework you have to do, etc. Try to avoid this! Your audience will be able to tell that you are mentally absent, and it will make your scene much less believable and spontaneous (and will certainly frustrate your partner!).

The beauty of acting is that it is slightly different every time, and if you stay attuned to those differences, your scene can unfold in a new and unique way every time you do it. For this reason, always remember to really see your partner when you look at him or her; really hear your partner when he or she speaks—and not just the words, but the vocal inflection, rhythm, facial expression, and body language.

The "W" Questions

Let's start by imagining that you are required to perform a *duet* scene from a Shakespeare play (a scene with two characters in it). Once you know what the scene is and who your scene partner will be, it is time to do some work on your own. You can just as easily apply these concepts to a *monologue* or soliloquy; simply leave out the partner work.

DUET

A song or scene involving two people.

MONOLOGUE

A speech, usually part of a play, that is performed by only one actor. Monologues are often required at auditions as a sample of an actor's work.

Read your scene over several times to make sure you have at least a basic understanding of it. Also make sure you have read the play it comes from at least once, so that you understand where your scene fits within the bigger picture of the play. Then, consider the following questions about your character and the scene, and write down your answers. Some of the answers will be provided for you by the play, but if you can't find them, don't worry; instead, make educated guesses based on what you already know of the character. Some of Shakespeare's characters are very clearly described, while others only show their characteristics through their actions and words.

1. *Who am I?* What is your character's name, social rank, occupation? How old is your character, and where is he or she from? How much education does your character have? What family relations does your character have? What is your character's relationship to the other character in the scene? How long have they known each other? What is your character wearing, and what does he or she look like? What are your character's likes, dislikes, hopes, and fears?

2. *What am I doing?* There will be the obvious, such as having a conversation with someone—but is your character also praying, hiding from someone, gardening, fighting a battle, or sewing? Does your character have to whisper or shout to be heard? What circumstances have brought you into this situation? What are you talking about with the other character?

3. *When is this happening?* What year is it, and how old is your character? What season is it? What day of the week? Is it a holiday? What time is it? Is it a mealtime? Are you hungry? What happened right before this scene?

4. *Where am I?* What country and city are you in? Are you outdoors, in a field, courtyard, park, or battlefield, or are you inside, in an alehouse, castle, bedroom, or barracks? Are you standing up, sitting down, or constantly moving? Are there other people around, or is it just the two of you? What else is in your environment (furniture, dishes, books, windows, doorways, etc.)? Where did you just come from?

5. *Why am I doing this?* Why are you here, with this person, discussing this subject? What do you hope to get out of it? What does your character expect will happen by the end of the scene? Do you want to be here, or are you here against your will? What are you trying to do to the other character?

6. *How will I do this?* How will you get the other character to do what you want, or how will you achieve your expectations from your "why" question? How will you overcome any obstacles along the way? Will you cajole, cry, beg, threaten, laugh, charm, or something else?

Once you have answered your "W" questions, compare them with your scene partner's answers. Discuss any differences, and then make the necessary changes so that any information that should agree, does agree (such as your relationship, your "where," your "when," etc.). Remember, strong, bold, active choices will be easier to play and more exciting to watch.

Text Work

Next, it's time to do your scansion. (If you need to refresh your memory about how to do scansion, go back and look at the section on scansion in chapter two of this book.) Once you have made a markup and written down a paraphrase, look at your partner's lines. Underline a word or phrase in each line that your character responds to. In other words, you are looking for the word in your partner's line that makes you say your next line. This is called the *cue line*. If you don't understand something your partner's character says, look at your partner's mark-up and paraphrase. As an example, let's look at a few lines between Richard III and Queen Anne, in Act I, Scene ii of *Richard III*. If you were playing Richard, you would want to choose the words in Anne's lines that give you your cue:

Cue Line

Usually the last line of an actor's speech, which is a signal to another performer that something else is to happen, such as another actor speaking, music starting, scenes changing, etc.

> ANNE: *O, he was <u>gentle</u>, <u>mild</u>, and <u>virtuous</u>.*
> RICHARD: *The better for the King of Heaven that hath him.*
> ANNE: *He is in <u>heaven</u>, where thou shalt never come.*
> RICHARD: *Let him thank me, that holp to send him thither,*
>   *For he was fitter for that place than earth.*

The cue line exercise will help you listen to your partner's lines more keenly, and to truly react to what your partner has to say rather than simply reading lines off a page. Remember that the word or words you have chosen in your partner's lines do not necessarily have to be the words they think are most important in their own scansion.

143

Table Work

Now that you have finished your text work, it is time to do your **table work**. Sit down with your scene partner (though you don't actually have to be sitting at

a table to do this), and start with a paraphrase reading. You will read the scene through, not with the original texts, but using your paraphrased text for your lines. As you do this, take your time. Really listen to what your partner is saying to you—it may change your understanding of your own lines, and therefore your paraphrase. If it does, simply let it. You don't have to read exactly what you have written on the page, but do try to stick to the sense of the original lines. Be sure to stay focused on your partner, making as much eye contact as possible. Don't forget to breathe. Repeat your paraphrase reading of the scene as many times as you need to until you both feel you really understand what is going on.

Next, you get to paraphrase each other's lines in a response paraphrase reading. Here's how it works: Take the original Shakespearean text of the scene. Whoever has the first line reads it, as slowly as necessary, to the second person. That second person then paraphrases what the first person has just said, and then says his own (Shakespearean) line in response. And it continues: You paraphrase whatever was said to you, and then say your own line back. Here's how a response paraphrase reading might go:

OPHELIA: *Good my lord,*
How does your honour for this many a day?

HAMLET: How've I been lately?
I humbly thank you: well, well, well.

OPHELIA: You thank me and tell me you've been fine.
My lord, I have remembrances of yours,
That I have longed long to re-deliver;
Pray you now, receive them.

HAMLET: You brought all the gifts and letters I gave you and you've wanted to give them back to me for a long time. You want me to take them back now.
No, not I; I never gave you aught.

OPHELIA: You deny giving me these letters and gifts!
My honour'd lord, you know right well you did....

You would continue that way through the rest of the scene. The response paraphrase reading helps ease you back into using Shakespeare's language to truly and honestly respond to one another in the scene. It also requires that you understand your partner's lines as well as you understand your own. And the better you understand your lines, the easier it will be to memorize them!

The last part of your table work involves simply reading the scene. But don't get lazy; this will require your full concentration and openness, so that you can still honestly respond to each other. The more you can do that, the more understandable and believable the scene will be. Remember, eye contact helps immensely when you are developing a scene, and you should know your script well enough by now that you won't have to depend on it too much anyway. You should only have to glance down occasionally. The "how" and "why" of your "W" questions will also help you here—as you read with your partner, remember what your character wants to get out of this scene and how he or she plans to get it.

Get the Scene on Its Feet

Now it's time for **blocking**. This is when the "where" part of your "W" questions will come in handy. Before you start deciding where and how your characters should move, set up your scene. Use as many actual props as you can—chairs, tables, windows, doors, and smaller things you might be able to bring in with you, such as dishes, books, or letters. Of course, you may not need many props at all; it just depends on where your scene is set or where you and your partner have chosen to set it.

BLOCKING

An actor's movement during a play, usually decided beforehand in rehearsal.

As you set up your "where," keep in mind the concept of stage picture. That is, when deciding how to move, you have to try to think like a member of the audience. They need to be able to see you (and, more specifically, your face) at all times. This doesn't mean that you and your partner must face stiffly forward the whole time; it just means that, while you move as naturally as possible, be careful not to block one another or turn your back on the audience completely.

STAGE DIRECTIONS

The vocabulary used to explain locations on a stage, usually for blocking purposes. Stage directions are usually given from the point of view of the actor facing the audience.

UPSTAGE

The part of the stage farthest from the audience.

DOWNSTAGE

The part of a stage closest to the audience.

STAGE RIGHT

The right part of a stage, as the actor faces the audience.

STAGE LEFT

The left part of a stage, as the actor faces the audience.

CENTER STAGE

The middle of the stage.

Before you plan how you will move during the scene, it may help to learn the vocabulary of blocking, known as *stage directions*. Think of these as points on a compass; using individual stage directions or combinations of them, you can identify almost any location on the stage.

The back of the stage, farthest from the audience, is called *upstage*, because stages used to slope upward, and therefore if you were standing at the back of it, you were literally higher up than if you were at the front. Using this same logic, the part of the stage closest to the audience is called *downstage*. *Stage right* and *stage left* are called so as you face the audience, and *center stage* is, of course, right in the middle. So, using these stage directions, a diagram of an empty stage would look like this:

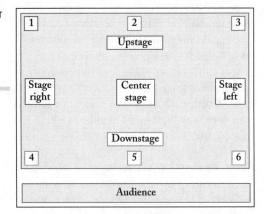

The numbered locations and their abbreviations are:

1. Upstage right (USR)   4. Downstage right (DSR)
2. Upstage center (USC)   5. Downstage center (DSC)
3. Upstage left (USL)   6. Downstage (DSL)

When you and your partner make decisions as to where each of them should move, you can make notations in your script using the abbreviations so that you don't forget them. A note such as "walk quickly DSL" or "enter SR" will help you to remember your blocking and solidify it quickly. This is not to say that you can't change blocking once you've set it. Sometimes it just doesn't work, and you have to stay put instead of moving to the other side of the stage, or vice versa.

Here are some tips that may help you with blocking:

- Generally, if the other person is speaking, you should be still.
- If you cross your partner on the stage (that is, walk past them), you should cross downstage of them if you are talking and upstage of them if they are talking (so that the person speaking is never blocked from the audience's view).
- Beware of being too close to your partner for a long period of time— it may cause you to speak so softly that you cannot be heard, and the audience doesn't feel as if it is being included on the action.
- Avoid pacing. If you must move a lot, do so only during the more emotional parts of the scene.
- At the same time, avoid being a statue. Even if your character is seated for the whole scene, you can still incorporate movement to make it interesting.
- Don't be afraid to use props as a way of adding movement to the scene. For some actors, a constant, regular movement helps them relax and focus on the scene. For instance, try playing solitaire, knitting, or peeling an orange. Use the context of the scene to help you decide what action might be appropriate.

Small Group ACTivity

Do a scene or monologue with action. You will need to have it memorized. Choose an activity to do while performing your scene—it can be folding laundry, lacing and unlacing a shoe, sewing, or separating and sorting money, for example. How does this action affect your acting? Does it make it more natural? Does it affect your character's emotions? Is it easier to do it with or without the action? If possible, try performing the scene or monologue for someone twice: once with the action, once without—and compare the two. **Scene Suggestions:** *Merchant of Venice,* Act II, Scene ii; *Two Gentlemen of Verona,* Act I Scene ii or Act II, Scene iii; *Richard III,* Act I, Scene i.

Memorizing Your Scene

OFF-BOOK

When an actor has memorized a script well enough that he no longer needs to look at it, he is off-book. During a rehearsal process, there is usually a deadline when all actors must be off-book. For a short period of time after that, they can still be prompted by the Assistant Stage Manager or glance at a nearby script if they forget a line.

If you intend to perform your scene *off-book*, now would be a good time to memorize it. Once you have blocked it, walking around and interacting physically becomes awkward if you have a script in your hand.

You might find the idea of memorizing an entire scene of Shakespeare daunting. Young actors are often worried that they won't be able to memorize their lines. But young minds are actually able to retain greater amounts of information more quickly than older minds are, so don't worry too much.

You have probably done enough table work that the text has already wormed its way into your memory anyway, the way you suddenly realize you know all the words to a new song on the radio without having consciously tried to learn them. All you have to do is a little extra work to make sure it stays in your memory.

If you are still concerned about memorizing lines, here are a few things that might help you:

- First, remember the musicality of Shakespeare's verse. All that rhythm, rhyme, and repeated sound can work to your advantage.

- Second, make sure you have a concrete image for every line or sentence. Then, use the words of that line to try to make your partner see that image. Not only will this make your acting clearer, it will help you to memorize large amounts of text at a time, because all you'll have to do is remember a series of images rather than a whole bunch of words.

- Third, don't try to do it all at once. When I have a script to memorize, I figure out the number of pages I have to learn and then divide it by the number of days until I have to be off-book; this gives me the number of pages I have to learn per day until I am no longer allowed to use my script. It isn't usually much—just two or three—and that makes it easier to handle.

- When all else fails, record! Using a blank cassette or CD, record yourself saying your lines and your partner's, then just your partner's with pauses for yours. You've basically created your own prompter!

Listen to it whenever you can until your lines have lodged themselves firmly in your brain.

Once you and your partner have memorized your scripts, ask a friend to be "on book" as you rehearse the scene. If you suddenly forget what comes next, all you have to do is say, "Line!" and your friend can read aloud the first few words of your line (this is called prompting). That should be enough to jog your memory so that you can finish the line yourself.

Small Group ACTivity

Choose a monologue or scene to act out. First, do it very dramatically: Deepen your voice, draw out your words, use big, expansive gestures and loud emotions. Then, try the same scene or monologue very naturally. Which is more difficult? Which seems more appropriate to the material? If you do it in front of an audience, which did they like better, and why? **Scene Suggestions:** *King Lear*, Act III, Scene ii; *Hamlet,* Act III, Scene iii; *Macbeth*, Act II, Scene i or ii.

A NOTE ABOUT NERVES

Reading or performing in front of your family, friends, and/or classmates can be scary sometimes. Remember that being a little nervous is good—it means that you care about what you're doing enough to want to do it well. But if you find yourself paralyzed by stage fright, there are steps you can take to combat it.

Exactly which steps you take depends on how your nerves manifest themselves. For instance, many people speak too quickly and trip over their words when they're nervous. To avoid this, you need to warm up your mouth. Choose a few of your lines to "speed through" five times, then move on to Shakespearean tongue twisters. A couple of useful tongue twisters:

- *But she as far surpasseth Sycorax as great'st doth least* (from *The Tempest*)
- *She doth teach the torches to burn bright* (from *Romeo and Juliet*)

Repeat each of those lines at least five times, speeding up as you go, and your mouth will be warmed up.

Another problem might be that you feel you can't speak loudly enough in front of a crowd. The solution to this is twofold. First, you must warm up your voice. If you know how to sing, hum a few scales. If not, go through your lines in a normal voice, enjoy a few good belly laughs (this will warm up your diaphragm, where your breath support comes from), then quietly slide your voice from the highest you can speak all the way down to the lowest you can speak. (*Never* scream—it will only hurt your voice.) Then when you start your scene, imagine your voice hitting the back wall of the room, even when your scene partner is standing close to you: this is known as vocal projection.

If you simply get tense or get butterflies in your stomach, some relaxation exercises might help. Close your eyes and do some deep breathing and neck rolls. Bring your shoulders up to your ears and drop them again several times. Then gently shake out your hands.

When it comes right down to it, remember that even the most seasoned performers get a little nervous; however, most learn to channel their nervousness into the physical energy and mental focus that are needed for a good performance. The best way to avoid being *too* nervous is to be prepared. If you have rehearsed well, you must trust yourself enough to have confidence in your performance.

Getting a Shakespeare Scene on its Feet: A Quick Summary

From start to finish, here is what to remember when preparing a scene for performance:

1. Use your own accent!
2. Make a "W" list.
3. Do a scansion markup and paraphrase your lines.
4. Underline the cues in your partner's text.
5. Do a paraphrase reading.
6. Do a response paraphrase reading.
7. Do an original text reading.
8. Set up your "where" and block the scene.
9. Memorize the scene.
10. Rehearse it as many times as you need to until you're ready!

❧ CHAPTER SEVEN ❧

GOING TO SEE SHAKESPEARE: WHY IT IS NOT LIKE WATCHING TV

These are the youths that thunder at a playhouse.
—*Henry VIII*, ACT V, SCENE IV, LINES 58–59

WHY NOT JUST SEE A MOVIE?

Much of this book has suggested seeing movies of Shakespeare's plays, and there is no denying that there are a lot of good Shakespeare films out there. But most of those suggestions were about focusing on one particular aspect of Shakespeare. If you want to truly experience Shakespeare's plays the way Shakespeare intended his plays to be experienced, nothing beats live *theatre*. Nothing.

THEATRE

A building (or outdoor structure) in which the live representation of an action or story takes place; also, the live representation of the story itself.

You might think there is no difference between going to the movies and going to the theatre. Nothing could be further from the truth, and there are many reasons why. But the main reason is that a movie is an event that has already happened, and you have no part in it. The actors have already made the movie, and whether you're watching it or not does not affect them one way or the other. But when you are at the theatre, you are very much a part of—even a participant in—the event that is taking place on stage. You may not think you make a difference, but you do.

In the theatre, the story is happening in real time, and you are right there, breathing the same air as the characters on stage. Just like a movie, you can hear them—but unlike a movie, or any other type of technological entertainment, *they can also hear you.* Film is very much a visual medium, but at the theatre, you use your other senses as well. Why else would people who watch TV be called *viewers*, while people who watch theatre are called an *audience*, as in "people who *hear*"? At the theatre, you can feel and experience the events right along with the characters onstage. At the movies, you watch passively; at the theatre, you participate actively.

VIEWER

One who watches movies or television; a passive observer rather than an active participant.

AUDIENCE

Literally, a group of people who are in the act of hearing something.

The fact is that, when you go to the theatre, you change it. Your very presence makes it a different performance than it would have been otherwise, because there is a very real exchange of energy between the actors and the audience that doesn't just happen during the applause. Actors are constantly aware of the audience, just as much as the audience is aware of the actors. An actor can be completely "in the moment" in terms of the lines he is delivering and the characters he is interacting with. But at the same time, he could tell you who in the audience has a cold, who is unable to sit still in their seat, and where the most raucous laughter is coming from. What it all comes down to is that the audience is a very important part of Shakespeare's plays.

Theatre as Ritual

As a modern, Western culture, we have lost much of our **ritual**. In societies of the past, people would come together for religious rituals. But now, because of religious freedom, we no longer share the same religious traditions, and therefore any religious rituals we have are only shared with the other members of our own religion, and not with society as a whole.

RITUAL

An act or series of acts repeatedly performed according to a specific custom.

Theatre is one of the few shared rituals we have left. Think about it: We all show up at a predetermined time, sacrifice money for a ticket, then sit together with many other people to observe other people on the stage going through a very carefully determined set of movements and saying words and singing songs that have been handed down to them through the ages. We know the places where we are expected to respond, and we do so accordingly by laughing or applauding.

Historically, the comparison of theatre to ritual is not much of a stretch, because theatre actually began as a religious ceremony in ancient Greece. The Greeks worshipped many gods, and many stories formed around the interactions between the gods and between gods and humans. At yearly festivals honoring the gods, people began dressing up as one deity or another and acting out these stories in front of other worshippers.

Since the days of the Greeks, the way we tell our stories has changed drastically. With the proliferation of television, computer games, and the Internet, our participation in these stories has become much more passive and solitary. When you watch a DVD or surf the Web, you often do so alone; there isn't much fellowship involved. But with theatre, fellowship is part of the point: It wouldn't make much sense for a whole cast and crew to put on a play for one person at a time! You have to be part of a crowd of people in order to experience theatre.

Shakespeare and Your History

Another great thing about going to see Shakespeare at the theatre is that it is an experience you share with thousands of people who have come before you. Your ancestors, famous historical figures, even the former leaders of your country may have gone to see Shakespeare's plays, no matter where or when they lived, because Shakespeare's plays are performed all over the world and have been for a long time. (And even if they never made it to the theatre, they might have read or heard the stories of Shakespeare.) As you sit in a darkened theatre, watching Shakespeare's stories unfold before you on the stage, this is food for thought: Your very own great-grandparent may have done this very same thing—performed this very same ritual—a hundred years ago. And a hundred years from now, your great-grandchildren may be continuing this tradition. So by seeing Shakespeare in a theatre, you are connecting yourself to your past, your future, or both.

HOW TO FIND LIVE SHAKESPEARE

You may already know of the theatres that perform Shakespeare in or near your community. And of course, there are always the obvious ways of finding local theatres, such as the arts and entertainment section of your local newspaper and the yellow pages in your phone book. But there are also a few resources on the Internet that you may find useful:

- If you're looking specifically for professional theatres that produce Shakespeare, try the Shakespeare Theatre Association of America. The STAA's website at *http://web.uvic.ca/shakespeare/STAA/*, has a membership directory, with member theatres all over the United States and Canada.

- Community theatres often perform at least one Shakespeare play during their season. The American Association of Community Theatres has a website at *www.aact.org*. On the "Member Companies" page, you can search for a theatre using the theatre name, a city, or a state. It will then give you a listing with the name of the theatre, the box office phone number, and the theatre's web address.

- Theatre Canada maintains a website listing all kinds of theatre around Canada—educational, community, and professional. Their website can be found at *www.theatrecanada.org/english/default.htm*.

- Universities and theatre schools are great places to find good, and often very affordable, Shakespeare. The University/Resident Theatre Association maintains a list of active members on their website, *www.URTA.com*. The National Association of Schools of Theatre has a search engine where you can plug in the name of a school, city, or state to see what members may be near you; their website is *http://nast.arts-accredit.org*.

If you are fortunate enough to have a lot of choices for seeing Shakespeare, try lots of different types of theatre settings to figure out what you like. Seeing a Shakespeare play in a park's amphitheatre is much different from seeing it in a small indoor theatre that seats 100, which is different still from seeing it in a large auditorium that seats 800 or 1,000. Each space will have its own unique quality, and you might want to experiment with each to discover which you like best.

GETTING (AND AFFORDING) A TICKET

Once you have found a company that performs Shakespeare, you'll want to buy a ticket. If you can afford a full-price ticket, great. Try to buy it ahead of time in case they sell out the night of the show.

But live theatre, especially professional theatre, can be very expensive, and sometimes it's hard to scrape together the money to buy a ticket. Don't worry; there are other ways of getting a ticket besides paying full price.

Fortunately, since many theatres' operating budgets are so tight, they are constantly in need of volunteers to help keep them running smoothly. Try calling the theatre a couple of weeks ahead of time and asking if there's anything you can do for them in exchange for a ticket. Many theatres will set you to work ushering; the night you go to the show, they might ask you to tear tickets, hand out programs, or show people to their seats. If they already have enough ushers, there are lots of other things they might need, such as stuffing envelopes for a mass mailing or sorting and organizing costumes. If you call a theatre to offer your services, chances are they won't turn you down and will be quite happy to have the extra help.

If for some strange reason the theatre doesn't need any extra help at the time, there are often ways to save money on a ticket. Many theatres offer student-level prices, but if those are still too expensive for you, ask whether the theatre offers student rush tickets. Student rush works like this: In the five or ten minutes before the show begins, the box office releases any unsold tickets for sale at a much lower price. You just have to get in line ahead of time and hope they don't sell out by the time it's your turn. Some theatres also offer pay-what-you-can nights. These usually occur on the last couple of dress rehearsals, which may be open to the public for a reduced price. On a pay-what-you-can night, there is sometimes a suggested donation amount, but you can pay more or less than the suggested donation, depending on what you can afford.

PREPARING TO SEE SHAKESPEARE

You may want to read a little bit of the play you are going to see, especially if you aren't familiar with it. But if you aren't already familiar with the story, don't make the mistake of reading the whole thing. One of the best things about Shakespeare is his stories, and if you don't know how this particular story ends, don't ruin it for yourself. Treat it like the latest action movie: How upset would you be if your best friend saw it and told you who the killer was before you had a chance to see the film? Try to think of Shakespeare the same way, and you'll have a whole new sense of wonder as you watch the story unfold unexpectedly before you.

Just to prepare yourself, read the first act of the play. Remember to follow the suggestions for reading Shakespeare in chapter two, starting with reading it out loud, not silently to yourself. This will help you get a sense of the language, so that it will be less of a shock to your brain when you hear it in the theatre. The other advantage is that it will give you a sense of the *exposition*—that is, what has happened in the characters' lives up to the point when the play starts. You'll also have a sense of the various characters involved, their relationships, and the world they live in. In fact, it would be beneficial to do some of the *Dramatis Personae* exercises from chapter two, so that you have a clear sense of who is who.

If you prepare yourself this way, you can lose yourself in the action of the play once you're there in the theatre.

Solo ACTivity

Keep a theatre journal. When you go to the theatre, bring a notebook and write down your impressions of what you see (remember not to write during the show; wait until intermission and afterward). You can write about your expectations as compared to what you see, how the actors bring the story to life, how the costumes, lighting, sound, and set add to or detract from the story, or anything else that interests you. Later, you'll have a permanent record of your experience at the theatre.

AT THE THEATRE

You may find it useful to get to the theatre about a half-hour before the show begins (of course, if you're ushering, this won't be an issue). This will give you ample time to deal with parking and picking up your tickets, and also to get settled in your seat and read the program. Many theatres publish photographs of the actors in their programs, so you may have a chance to familiarize yourself with their faces so that you know who is playing whom when the show starts.

People often worry about what to wear to the theatre. Wear whatever you are comfortable sitting in for a couple of hours. You will see people who are dressed up, in suits or dresses. If you want to do this, go ahead, but you should never feel bad about wearing whatever is available (assuming it is clean and presentable). Just remember that everybody is there to see the show, not you.

Every theatre has its own set of "house policies." House policies are just that particular theatre's set of rules for audience behavior. Although the rules listed below are often included in a theatre's house policies, they are good to observe whether they're listed or not.

1. Before you enter the theatre, turn your cell phone and pager off and disable your beeping watch (or better yet, leave them at home). The ring of a cell phone or pager during a performance will not only be extremely annoying to your fellow audience members, it will also absolutely shatter the concentration of the actors onstage.

2. Don't bring a camera, tape recorder, or camcorder. In fact, taping a show without permission can be illegal. Going to the theatre is certainly an experience you'll want to remember, but rely on your own memory, not a tape.

3. Don't talk during the show. It is easy to forget that while the actors on stage may be giving a flawless performance that reminds you of seeing a movie, they are not merely projections on a screen—they are real, live people who can get distracted when they hear you whispering out in the audience.

4. Sometimes when audience members have coughs or colds, they like to bring cough drops or hard candy with them. If you need to bring that sort of thing along, make sure it's the type wrapped in waxed paper (rather than loud, crackly cellophane) and that you unwrap what you need before the show starts. Avoid chewing gum.

5. If you're sitting in an aisle seat, keep your hands and feet out of the aisles. Sometimes actors use the aisles for entrances onto the stage, and when it's dark, it's hard for them to see and avoid obstacles that could trip them.

Most of these rules seem obvious, but you would be amazed at how many people don't bother to follow them. It is very important to remember that you are not at the movies or in your own home and that the actors and your fellow audience members deserve your respect.

Solo ACTivity

After reading and seeing a Shakespeare play live, choose which character you would most like to play. Then try calling the theatre and asking if you can conduct an interview with the actor who played that character (some may prefer that you to leave your phone number so the actor can contact you). The actor may be willing to talk to you about what it's like to play that character and the process they have gone through to portray the role. Then, either write a summary about what you have learned or prepare a monologue or scene of the character using what you have learned from that actor.

Fitting In at the "Theatah"

One of the funny things about the way Shakespeare is thought of today is that people often lump Shakespearean theatre into the same groups as the ballet or the opera—"elitist" pastimes rather than popular entertainment. After all, season ticket holders vie for opening night seats at Shakespeare festivals the way they do for the symphony, and they dress in their finery when the big night comes.

If Shakespeare saw us treating his plays this way, he would probably laugh. He would certainly be surprised. During Shakespeare's lifetime, servants and beggars attended his plays more often than royalty did. Sure, the plays were often performed in a theatre—but they were also performed in city streets, using boards laid across two barrels for a stage, and in fields or roadside taverns from the back of a wagon that served as a performance space. Shakespeare's plays were never meant to be lofty or snooty or exclusive or even very sophisticated—and they shouldn't be today, either. There are even fart jokes in Shakespeare. When was the last time you heard about a fart joke in a ballet?

So if you're concerned about feeling uncomfortable at the theatre, don't be. Don't feel as if it's a place where you don't belong, or that you are somehow not good enough or smart enough to be there. Shakespeare's plays are for everybody.

IF YOU CAN'T FIND LIVE SHAKESPEARE

As important as it is to see Shakespeare live onstage, it may simply not be possible for you. You may live in a community that has no live theatre, and you may not live close enough to a bigger city that may have it. If this is the case, there is a wealth of Shakespeare on film. Just remember that film cannot be a replacement for live theatre, as it is a completely different medium. Think of film as an alternative when you can't see live theatre. Your local video rental store may have some Shakespeare plays on film, and libraries are also a great resource. Additionally, your local public television channel (PBS) may occasionally show versions of Shakespeare's plays. The PBS website, *www.pbs.org*, has a search engine to find what's showing on your local channel. Appendix B lists some of the films that have been made of Shakespeare's plays, so you'll know what to look for.

Small Group ACTivity

Watch the 1967 and 1996 film versions of *Romeo and Juliet* (or any other two filmed versions of one play; see Appendix B). Discuss how they compare and contrast. Some things to concentrate on are casting choices, script adaptation, setting, camera angles, speed (pace), and costumes.

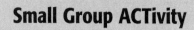

Small Group ACTivity

Host a Shakespearean film festival in your classroom or home (refer to Appendix B for ideas). Invite your family and/or friends. Write up expositions (or summaries of the first act) they can refer to before watching.

SHAKESPEARE OF YOUR OWN

And of course, there is no rule that says you can't put on your own performance of Shakespeare. It's really not as difficult as you might think. You don't need an operating budget, just a large room with some chairs. It can be as simple or as elaborate as you choose to make it.

Although producing a Shakespeare play can be quite an undertaking, you can do it with a little help from your friends or family. Listed below are some of the more important points to take into consideration:

1. What to perform? You could do a whole play, or if you would prefer, a series of scenes. An evening of monologues and scenes from various Shakespeare plays can be very entertaining and allows the audience see a variety of styles and actors. If you choose to do a whole play, remember that you'll want to cut it down first, as many of Shakespeare's plays are about 4 hours long, uncut. To cut a play, look for dialogue and scenes that don't contribute directly to the action of the play.

2. Where to perform and rehearse? As stated above, you don't need a state-of-the-art, 800-seat performing arts center. Just about any room will do, whether it's a converted classroom, a church basement, or a community center conference room. If it happens to have a raised platform at one end that can be used as a stage, great; if not, make the best of whatever space you do have. Remember that you can do theatre outdoors, too, if the weather is warm. Your local parks department may even know of the existence of an amphitheatre. Rehearsals don't have to take place in the same space you perform in—again, classrooms are great, as are living rooms and backyards. (Just remember to ask whomever the space belongs to if you can use it.)

3. How long to rehearse? That depends on the availability of your actors and your rehearsal space. If your actors are available in the afternoons or evenings after school, or during lunch, great; you can rehearse every day and have the play ready in three to six weeks. If you're pressed for rehearsal time, a ***staged reading*** is a good alternative. A staged reading is just like a play, with full blocking, but the actors carry around their scripts just in case they need them. Remember that you can rehearse the play in bits and pieces, and that way not every actor will be needed every day.

> **STAGED READING**
>
> A performance with full blocking, but the actors carry around their scripts. Sets and costumes may or may not be used.

4. What about directing and casting? You will need someone who watches rehearsals with an objective eye and can create an overall arc to the performance. You can direct it yourself (although if you do, I recommend not being in the play as well), or ask a teacher, parent, or classmate to direct. They can keep rehearsals running smoothly and direct the blocking to create stage pictures. Casting the production can be as elaborate as holding auditions and assigning roles based on them, or as simple as asking for volunteers: "Who wants to play Juliet?" Remember that boys don't always have to play boys' roles, and vice versa: If you have all girls, an all-girl production of a Shakespeare play can be very interesting and effective. Also, you can double up on roles: any actor can play two or three characters, provided none of those characters are in any scenes together.

5. What about costumes? Costumes can be wonderfully simple. Once the cast begins to get familiar with their characters, ask them to go to their closet as that character and pick out what the character would most like to wear. A queen might like a prom dress or business suit; a merchant may prefer khakis and a collared shirt; Hamlet may be most comfortable in ripped jeans and a T-shirt. If you want to and are able to add such accessories as sword belts or crowns, do so. If any actors are playing more than one character, the costume change can be as simple as putting on a different hat or jacket.

Producing a Shakespeare play is never a minor task; however, the beauty of Shakespeare's language will shine through if you keep things simple. If you have a large budget, a lot of volunteers with expertise, and large amounts of time, you can certainly put on a more elaborate production, but you should never feel that you won't be doing justice to the plays by keeping things simple. If you pay attention to the acting and the poetry, you don't need fancy costumes, or complex lighting, or detailed sets; the language will speak for itself.

Solo ACTivity

Imagine that you are a sound designer for a theatre. Choose a Shakespeare play and create your own soundtrack for it. There should be at least one song for each of the following: background music to play while the audience takes their seats in the theatre, music for the opening of the curtain at the beginning of the play, music to introduce each major character, and music to play during the curtain call when the actors take their bows. Choose each song carefully to fit the mood and setting of the play and the personality of the character, then put them all onto a CD or tape. Write some notes that list the title and artist of each song and that explain a little bit about why you chose each song for each purpose.

Section Four

APPENDICES

FAMOUS LINES FROM SHAKESPEARE

This is a collection of the most famous lines from Shakespeare. Many of these have found their way into regular speech. There is room at the end to write your own favorite lines as you study Shakespeare.

Antony and Cleopatra

"My salad days, when I was green in judgment." (Act I, Scene v)

As You Like It

"All the world's a stage, and all the men and women merely players. They have their exits and their entrances; And one man in his time plays many parts." (Act II, Scene vii)

"True is it that we have seen better days." (Act II, Scene vii)

"Can one desire too much of a good thing?" (Act IV, Scene i)

"For ever and a day." (Act IV, Scene i)

"The fool doth think he is wise, but the wise man knows himself to be a fool." (Act V, Scene i)

Cymbeline

"The game is up." (Act III, Scene iii)

"I have not slept one wink." (Act III, Scene iii)

Hamlet

"Frailty, thy name is woman!" (Act I, Scene ii)

"Neither a borrower nor a lender be." (Act I, Scene iii)

"This above all: to thine own self be true." (Act I, Scene iii)

Hamlet (continued)

"That it should come to this!" (Act I, Scene ii)

"In my mind's eye." (Act I, Scene ii)

"The play's the thing wherein I'll catch the conscience of the king." (Act II, Scene ii)

"Though this be madness, yet there is method in 't." (Act II, Scene ii)

"What a piece of work is man! How noble in reason! How infinite in faculty! in form and moving how express and admirable! in action how like an angel! in apprehension how like a god! The beauty of the world, the paragon of animals!" (Act II, Scene ii)

"To be, or not to be: that is the question." (Act III, Scene i)

"Ay, there's the rub." (Act III, Scene i)

"The lady doth protest too much, methinks." (Act III, Scene ii)

"Good night, sweet prince: and flights of angels sing thee to thy rest!" (Act V, Scene ii)

Henry IV, Part I

"He will give the devil his due." (Act I, Scene ii)

"The better part of valour is discretion." (Act V, Scene iv)

Henry IV, Part II

"He hath eaten me out of house and home." (Act II, Scene i)

"Uneasy lies the head that wears a crown." (Act III, Scene i)

"A man can die but once." (Act III, Scene ii)

Henry V

"Once more unto the breach, dear friends, once more, or close the wall up with our English dead!" (Act III, Scene i)

"Men of few words are the best men." (Act III, Scene ii)

"We few, we happy few, we band of brothers." (Act IV, Scene iii)

Henry VI, Part II

"Smooth runs the water where the brook is deep." (Act III, Scene ii)

"The first thing we do, let's kill all the lawyers." (Act IV, Scene ii)

Henry VI, Part III

"Having nothing, nothing can he lose." (Act III, Scene iii)

Julius Caesar

"Beware the Ides of March." (Act I, Scene ii)

"But, for my own part, it was Greek to me." (Act I, Scene ii)

"A dish fit for the gods." (Act II, Scene i)

"Cry 'Havoc,' and let slip the dogs of war." (Act III, Scene i)

"Et tu, Brute!" (Act III, Scene i)

"Friends, Romans, countrymen, lend me your ears; I come to bury Caesar, not to praise him." (Act III, Scene ii)

King Lear

"Nothing will come of nothing." (Act I, Scene i)

"Have more than thou showest, speak less than thou knowest, lend less than thou owest." (Act I, Scene iv)

"I am a man more sinned against than sinning." (Act III, Scene ii)

Macbeth

"When shall we three meet again in thunder, lightning, or in rain? When the hurlyburly's done, when the battle's lost and won." (Act I, Scene i)

"Yet do I fear thy nature; It is too full o' the milk of human kindness." (Act I, Scene v)

"Is this a dagger which I see before me, The handle toward my hand?" (Act II, Scene i)

"There's daggers in men's smiles." (Act II, Scene iii)

"Double, double toil and trouble; Fire burn, and cauldron bubble." (Act IV, Scene i)

Macbeth (continued)

"Out, damned spot! out, I say!" (Act V, Scene i)

"I bear a charmed life." (Act V, Scene viii)

"Out, out, brief candle! Life's but a walking shadow, a poor player that struts and frets his hour upon the stage and then is heard no more: it is a tale told by an idiot, full of sound and fury, signifying nothing." (Act V, Scene v)

Measure for Measure

"Our doubts are traitors, and make us lose the good we oft might win, by fearing to attempt." (Act I, Scene iv)

The Merchant of Venice

"Love is blind, and lovers cannot see the pretty follies that they themselves commit." (Act II, Scene vi)

"If you prick us, do we not bleed? if you tickle us, do we not laugh? if you poison us, do we not die? and if you wrong us, shall we not revenge?" (Act III, Scene i)

"The quality of mercy is not strained." (Act IV, Scene i)

The Merry Wives of Windsor

"Why, then the world's mine oyster." (Act II, Scene ii)

"This is the short and the long of it." (Act II, Scene ii)

"I cannot tell what the dickens his name is." (Act III, Scene ii)

"As good luck would have it." (Act III, Scene v)

A Midsummer Night's Dream

"The course of true love never did run smooth." (Act I, Scene i)

"Love looks not with the eyes, but with the mind, and therefore is winged Cupid painted blind." (Act I, Scene i)

"Lord, what fools these mortals be!" (Act III, Scene ii)

Othello

"I will wear my heart upon my sleeve." (Act I, Scene i)

"O, beware, my lord, of jealousy; it is the green-eyed monster which doth mock the meat it feeds on." (Act III, Scene iii)

"'Tis neither here nor there." (Act IV, Scene iii)

Richard III

"Now is the winter of our discontent." (Act I, Scene i)

"Off with his head!" (Act III, Scene iv)

"A horse! a horse! my kingdom for a horse!" (Act V, Scene iv)

Romeo and Juliet

"O Romeo, Romeo! wherefore art thou Romeo?" (Act II, Scene ii)

"But soft! What light through yonder window breaks? It is the east, and Juliet is the sun." (Act II, Scene ii)

"Good Night, Good night! Parting is such sweet sorrow, that I shall say good night till it be morrow." (Act II, Scene ii)

"What's in a name? That which we call a rose by any other name would smell as sweet." (Act II, Scene ii)

"A plague o' both your houses!" (Act III, Scene i)

"O, I am fortune's fool!" (Act III, Scene i)

Taming of the Shrew

"I'll not budge an inch." (Induction, Scene i)

"This is a way to kill a wife with kindness." (Act IV, Scene i)

The Tempest

"We are such stuff as dreams are made on." (Act IV, Scene i)

"O brave new world, that has such people in 't!" (Act V, Scene i)

Twelfth Night

"If music be the food of love, play on." (Act I, Scene i)

"Be not afraid of greatness: some are born great, some achieve greatness and some have greatness thrust upon 'em." (Act II, Scene v)

"Love sought is good, but giv'n unsought is better." (Act III, Scene i)

"For the rain it raineth every day." (Act V, Scene i)

My Favorite Lines from Shakespeare

Play	Act	Scene	Line

AN ANNOTATED LIST OF SHAKESPEARE'S PLAYS ON FILM

Since a list like this can get ridiculously long, no more than three filmed versions of each play are listed here. When possible, the list features movies from a range of time periods that involve either good or well-known actors (since, as we all know, those two qualities are not necessarily the same) or interesting settings, or some combination of the two. At the end are lists of adaptations of and films inspired by Shakespeare.

If the "Rating" category says "TV," it means that the film was made for television and does not bear a regular movie rating—but obviously, if it is shown on television, it is most likely appropriate for all audiences. If it says "NR," it is because the movie was made before the rating system came into being, but you can make the same assumption about its appropriateness.

Remember that if your local video store doesn't have what you're looking for, your library might. Also remember that seeing Shakespeare on film is nothing like seeing it in the live theatre, so you should always choose the latter if at all possible. If you ever want to know all the films that have ever been made of a Shakespeare play, check out the Internet Movie Database, at www.imdb.com. It's an excellent resource.

Title	Rating	Studio	Year	Director	Actor(s)	Notes
Antony and Cleopatra	NR	Folio Films	1973	Charlton Heston	Charlton Heston	Filmed in Spain, with epic naval battle sequences.
	TV	Incorporated Television Co.	1974	John Scoffield	Patrick Stewart, Ben Kingsley	A film adaptation of the Royal Shakespeare Company's stage production.
Hamlet	R	Double A Films	2000	Michael Almereyda	Ethan Hawke, Julia Stiles, Bill Murray	Set in modern-day New York City; "Denmark" is a corporation, not a country.
	PG-13	Castle Rock Entertainment	1996	Kenneth Branagh	Kenneth Branagh, Kate Winslet	Set in 19th century Europe—this one's 4 hours long.
	NR	Pilgrim Pictures	1948	Laurence Olivier	Laurence Olivier	Won Best Film and Best Actor (Olivier) at the Academy Awards.
	PG-13	BBC	1989	Kenneth Branagh	Kenneth Branagh, Derek Jacobi, Ian Holm	By showing how horrific medieval warfare was, Branagh's version manages to be anti-war.
Henry V	NR	Two Cities Films	1944	Laurence Olivier	Laurence Olivier	Shows what it would be like to see *Henry V* at the Globe Theatre in 1600.
Julius Caesar	NR	MGM	1953	Joseph L. Mankiewicz	Marlon Brando, John Gielgud	Brando won an Academy Award for his performance as Antony.
	TV	NY Shakespeare Festival	1979	Michael Langham	Morgan Freeman	A film of the stage version in the park.
	TV	BBC	1979	Herbert Wise	Richard Pasco, Charles Gray	The BBC made a television production of every Shakespeare play.

Title	Rating	Studio	Year	Director	Actor(s)	Notes
King Lear	TV	Granada Television	1984	Michael Elliot	Laurence Olivier, Diana Rigg	Olivier's last Shakespearean role on film.
	NR	Filmways Pictures	1971	Peter Brook	Paul Scofield, Anne-Lise Gabold	A bleak, pared-down version of the play.
	TV	NY Shakespeare Festival, PBS	1974	Edwin Sherin	James Earl Jones, Raul Julia	A film of Shakespeare in the park.
Macbeth	NR	Literary Classics Productions	1948	Orson Welles	Orson Welles	Categorized as "film noir," Welles' version captures the darkest side of the play.
	TV	Royal Shakespeare Co.	1979	Philip Casson (Trevor Nunn)	Ian McKellan, Judi Dench	A film adaptation of the RSC's stage version.
The Merchant of Venice	TV	PBS	2001	Trevor Nunn	Derbhle Crotty, Henry Goodman	Set in 1930's German cabaret era.
	TV	Associated Television	1973	Jonathan Miller	Laurence Olivier	Set in the early 1900s.
A Midsummer Night's Dream	PG-13	Fox Searchlight Productions	1999	Michel Hoffman	Kevin Kline, Michelle Pfeiffer, Calista Flockhart	Set in Tuscany in the late 19th century.
	TV	Filmways Pictures	1968	Peter Hall	Diana Rigg, Judi Dench, Ian Holm	Very stylized; shot completely with a hand-held camera.
	BBC	1981		Elijah Moshinsky	Phil Daniels, Cherith Mellor	Explores the darker, more sinister side of this normally light, silly comedy.

Title	Rating	Studio	Year	Director	Actor(s)	Notes
Much Ado About Nothing	PG-13	BBC/ Samuel Goldwyn	1993	Kenneth Branagh	Kenneth Branagh, Keanu Reeves, Denzel Washington	Branagh, as Benedick, and Emma Thompson, as Beatrice, were married at the time this was made.
	TV	BBC	1967	Alan Cooke, Franco Zeffirelli	Derek Jacobi, Maggie Smith	Franco Zeffirelli is probably best known for his version of *Romeo and Juliet*.
Othello	R	Castle Rock Entertainment	1995	Oliver Parker	Kenneth Branagh, Laurence Fishburne	Fishburne, though not known as a Shakespearean actor, comes into his own as Othello.
	NR	BHE Films	1965	Stuart Burge, John Dexter	Laurence Olivier, Maggie Smith	Olivier plays Othello.
	TV	BBC	1981	Jonathan Miller	Anthony Hopkins	Hopkins plays the title role.
Richard III	R	United Artists	1995	Richard Loncraine	Ian McKellan, Annette Benning, Robert Downey Jr.	Set in 1930's fascist Europe.
	TV	BBC	1983	Jane Howell	Ron Cook, Rowena Cooper	Part of a series of all of Shakespeare's War of the Roses plays.
	NR	London Film Productions	1955	Laurence Olivier	Laurence Olivier, John Gielgud	Considered to be Olivier's best work.
	NR	Kino Video	1912	James Keane, Andre Calmetes	Frederick Warde, Robert Gemp	Silent, hand-tinted, and the oldest surviving American feature film.

Title	Rating	Studio	Year	Director	Actor(s)	Notes
Romeo and Juliet	PG	BHE Films	1968	Franco Zeffirelli	Leonard Whiting, Olivia Hussey	In Italian, dubbed in English.
	PG-13	20th Century Fox	1996	Baz Luhrmann	Leonardo Di Caprio, Claire Danes	Set in fictitious Verona Beach, Florida.
	TV	BBC	1978	Alvin Rakoff	John Gielgud, Alan Rickman	Of special note is Alan Rickman's performance as Tybalt.
Taming of the Shrew	NR	FAI	1967	Franco Zeffirelli	Elizabeth Taylor, Richard Burton	Features a huge cast and lavish sets and costumes.
Titus	R	Clear Blue Sky Productions	1999	Julie Taymor	Anthony Hopkins	Set in ancient Rome, with modern touches.
Twelfth Night	PG	Rennaissance Films	1996	Trevor Nunn	Helena Bonham Carter, Ben Kingsley	This film shows the twins before the shipwreck, establishing their relationship vividly.
	TV	BBC	1980	John Gorrie	Alec McCowen, Felicity Kendal	A very basic, straightforward version of the play.

Appendix B

Adaptations

Based On	Title	Rated	Studio	Year	Director	Actor(s)	Notes
King Lear	The King of Texas	TV	TNT	2002	Uli Edel	Patrick Stewart	Set in the Old West during a battle over a rancher's land.
A Midsummer Night's Dream	Get Over It	PG-13	Miramax	2001	Tommy O'Haver	Kirsten Dunst, Sisqo, Martin Short	Another high school setting, but this on has a play-within-a-play at the end: the drama department is presenting "Dream."
Macbeth	Scotland, PA	R	Abandon Pictures	2001	Billy Morrissette	Maura Tierney, Christopher Walken, Andy Dick	A dark comedy set in 1975.
	Throne of Blood	NR	Toho Company Limited	1957	Akira Kurosawa		Set among Japanese samurai.
Othello	O	R	Miramax	2001	Tim Blake Nelson	Julia Stiles, Josh Hartnett, Brandy	Othello in a high school basketball team setting.
Taming of the Shrew	Kiss Me Kate	NR	MGM	1953	George Sidney	Bob Fosse	A musical version by Cole Porter.
	10 Things I Hate About You	PG-13	Touchstone Pictures	1999	Gil Junger	Julia Stiles, Heath Ledger, Joseph Gordon-Levitt	Takes place in a high school.

Adaptations, cont'd

Based On	Title	Rated	Studio	Year	Director	Actor(s)	Notes
Romeo and Juliet	*West Side Story*	NR	Beta Productions	1961	Jerome Robbins, Robert Wise	Natalie Wood	A musical version by Leonard Bernstein; the warring "families" are rival street gangs.
The Tempest	*Tempest*	PG	Columbia Pictures	1982	Paul Mazursky	Susan Sarandon, Raul Julia, Molly Ringwald	A modern-day *Tempest*, set partly in the Greek islands.
	Forbidden Planet	G	MGM	1956	Fred M. Wilcox	Leslie Nielsen	Science fiction Shakespeare, set in space.

Inspired by Shakespeare

Title	Rated	Studio	Year	Director	Actor(s)	Notes
The Complete Works of William Shakespeare, Abridged	TV	Acorn Media Group	2000	Paul Kafno	Adam Long, Reed Martin, Austin Tichenor	A film of a hilarious stage production—3 guys perform all 37 plays in under 2 hours.
Looking for Richard	PG-13	20th Century Fox	1996	Al Pacino	Al Pacino, Alec Baldwin, Kevin Spacey	A documentary about the problems of acting Shakespeare in general and Richard III in particular.
Shakespeare in Love	R	Miramax	1998	John Madden	Gwyneth Paltrow, Joseph Fiennes, Ben Affleck	A fictional account of what Shakespeare's life might have been like in the London theatre.

ACTivities Listed

SOLO ACTIVITIES

Chapter One

Page 8

Pretend you are Shakespeare, writing plays or movie scripts for today's actors. Which of today's stars could be depended upon to successfully play a certain character type (clown, king, villain, ingénue, etc.)? If necessary, consult chapter four, "Shakespeare's Characters." List at least three of each, then decide which combinations of actors would work best together.

Page 15

Compare the society you live in to Elizabethan England. The left-hand column of the chart on page 15 lists some of the aspects of Elizabethan society. How does your society compare? Fill in the right-hand column for each point.

Page 21

Create a timeline of Shakespeare's life. Using one color or set of symbols, show the significant dates in Shakespeare's life, as well as the approximate dates of each of his plays, when the Globe Theatre was erected, etc. Using a different color or set of symbols, show significant dates in the life of Elizabethan England: the defeat of the Spanish Armada, the plagues, the founding of the American colony of Virginia, and Elizabeth's death, just to name a few. Make the timeline as big as you would like, so that it is easy to read, and be as creative as you can—use magazine cutouts, draw your own pictures, or use computer graphics, for example.

Page 22

Choose one of these two projects to work on: Draw a map of Elizabethan London showing the location of the Old Globe and other landmarks, or build a three-dimensional model of the Globe theatre. For the map, you may make it as large and detailed as you like. For the model, you may build it out of whatever material you like; just be sure to show the three tiers of gallery seating, the pit, and the location of the stage.

Page 24

Be a costume designer. Imagine that you are in charge of designing costumes for a modern-day theatre company, but that they want to see drawings of costumes for both Elizabethan dress and contemporary dress.

Choose a character from any Shakespeare play, and do some research. What would this character have worn had he or she lived in Elizabethan times? Do a sketch, complete with colors, of what the costume should look like. For the contemporary costume, research fashion magazines and clothing catalogs, and think, "If this character were alive right now, what would he or she wear?" Do another color sketch of the contemporary costume.

Chapter Two

Page 37

Choose two scenes from two different plays. Read one scene out loud once; read the other silently to yourself once. Then, try to write a detailed summary of each scene. Which scene is easier to remember? Why?

Page 40

Choose a Shakespearean play and, using the Dramatis Personae, make a chart of all the characters. You can draw a picture of each character, use colors to tell them apart, or use abstract symbols to denote each character. Make sure your chart also shows the relationship between the characters. Then, read the play (or one act or scene of it) and see whether your chart helped your understanding of the play. If you need to, go back to your chart and make any required changes or additions as you read the play, based on what you've learned about the characters.

Page 47

What would Shakespeare sound like if he wrote today? Translate a scene of your choice from a Shakespearean play. Use the language you use every day to put the scene into your own words while fully retaining the meaning. Feel free to use slang, but not profanity. **Scene Suggestions:** *Romeo and Juliet*, Act I, Scene i; *As You Like It*, Act I, Scene iii; *Hamlet*, Act III, Scene i.

Chapter Three

Page 62

The next time you sit down to watch your favorite sitcom or TV drama, take some notes on the plot and subplot. Does the episode tell only one story, or does it interweave two or more? Does the subplot parallel the main plot? How? If the main plot is funny, is the subplot sad, or vice versa? Are any characters involved in both plots? How are the plot and subplot resolved?

Page 67

Many of Shakespeare's plays were based on popular, well-known stories or parts of history. If he were writing today, what stories would he use? Write a scene from a "current" Shakespeare play based on a popular, well-known story such as an urban legend, popular movie, or news item. Don't forget to give your new play a name! **Large Group Variation:** Act out the scene from the "new" Shakespeare play for an audience, then discuss with them how it compared to the original story and what kind of artistic license you took.

Page 68

Write a short story of your own based on the story of Pyramus and Thisbe. Would you choose to modernize it at all? What misunderstandings will you create to lead up to a tragic, ironic conclusion? Could you instead create misunderstandings to lead up to a comic conclusion? Read your finished story and the original Pyramus and Thisbe again, and make notes on the comparison. What parts of the original story did you keep? What did you change, and why?

Page 77

Choose a scene from one of Shakespeare's tragedies or histories and rewrite it, taking out all the conflict. What happens to the plot? Would the play be shorter or longer if all the conflict was missing? Would it be interesting to watch? What effect does conflict have on the plots of plays? **Scene Suggestions:** *Romeo and Juliet,* Act III, Scene i; *Othello,* Act IV, Scene i; *King Lear,* Act I, Scene i.

Chapter Four

Page 88

Choose the character type that you think is most opposite of your personality (your choice doesn't have to match your gender). Choose a monologue or scene to perform for the class. Discuss whether it was harder or easier to play a character that was not at all like you. Ask the class whether it was convincing.

Page 92

Make a description list for any character of your choosing. List the adjectives and verbs that best describe that character, both physically and psychologically, and using your list, decide what character category he or she belongs in. If you like, prepare a monologue or scene with the help of your description list.

Chapter Six

Page 139

Watch two different productions of the same Shakespeare play and compare the two. Ideally, try and make at least one of them a live production. If both are movies, try to get them from different time periods, such as Laurence Olivier's *Hamlet* (1948) and Ethan Hawke's *Hamlet* (2000) (see Appendix B for a list of Shakespeare on film). Compare the acting styles of the various actors. Which seems more believable to you, and why? What do they have in common? How does the setting of the play (where and when it takes place) affect the acting and the story?

Chapter Seven

Page 156

Keep a theatre journal. When you go to the theatre, bring a notebook and write down your impressions of what you see (remember not to write during the show; wait until intermission and afterward). You can write about your expectations as compared to what you see, how the actors bring the story to life, how the costumes, lighting, sound, and set add to or detract from the story, or anything else that interests you. Later, you'll have a permanent record of your experience at the theatre.

Page 158

After reading and seeing a Shakespeare play live, choose which character you would most like to play. Then try calling the theatre and asking if you can conduct an interview with the actor who played that character (some may prefer that you to leave your phone number so the actor can contact you). The actor may be willing to talk to you about what it's like to play that character and the process they have gone through to portray the role. Then, either write a summary about what you have learned or prepare a monologue or scene of the character using what you have learned from that actor.

Page 162

Imagine that you are a sound designer for a theatre. Choose a Shakespeare play and create your own soundtrack for it. There should be at least one song for each of the following: background music to play while the audience takes their seats in the theatre, music for the opening of the curtain at the beginning of the play, music to introduce each major character, and music to play during the curtain call when the actors take their bows. Choose each song carefully to fit the mood and setting of the play and the personality of the character, then put them all onto a CD or tape. Write some notes that list the title and artist of each song and that explain a little bit about why you chose each song for each purpose.

SMALL GROUP ACTIVITIES

Chapter One

Page 6

Imagine that you are writing a short biography of a historical person, but that you have very limited information on that person. In fact, the only things you know about that person are the following:

- His name was Jonathan Sumner.
- He was born on November 14, 1922 in Atlanta, Georgia.
- He attended Washington University in St. Louis.
- He married Jane Galbraith on March 22, 1944.
- He had three children: Katherine, Michael, and Walter.
- He moved to Los Angeles, California in 1950 and rented a house there.
- He wrote three books about the U.S. Civil War under a different name.
- He died in Los Angeles on November 18, 1970 and is buried there.

Based on this information, write a short (one- or two-page) biography of Jonathan Sumner, filling in the gaps for information you don't know based on what you think would be likely. When you're finished, compare your short biography of Jonathan Sumner with those of your friends. What information is different? Were any of your conjectures the same? What were your friends' reasons for filling in the gaps the way they did?

Page 11

With a partner, choose any two-person scene from a Shakespeare play. Decide which character you will play, then hand-write your own sides from the script. Remember, a side consists of only your lines, with a few words from the end of your partner's lines to prompt you. Act out the scene using your sides, then act out the scene using regular scripts. Discuss which one was easier and why.

Page 18

Imagine that it is possible to be elected to the office of Mayor of London in Elizabethan England, and that you are running for that position. The election is coming up soon, and you have to establish your platform and write a campaign speech. What will you promise to change? What morals and values will you promise to uphold? For instance, what will you tell the voters about Protestants, Catholics, and humanists? What will you say about the plague? In what ways will you promise to support Queen Elizabeth?

Decide on your platform and write your campaign speech. (If you design any other campaign materials, such as posters, remember that most of your voters are illiterate.) Deliver your campaign speech to your friends and family.

Page 25

Choose a short scene (or part of a scene) from a Shakespeare play that takes place in a specific setting: on a beach, in a tavern, in a great hall, on the castle battlements. Perform it once for your friends or family without telling them where it is, and see if they can get a sense of the setting just by watching you. Then, create as much of the scene as you possibly can: draw scenery on the blackboard or large sheets of paper, and use furniture and other props. Play the scene for your audience again and discuss the differences. Was it easier for you to act in the scene when you had a concrete environment? When your audience members could only envision the setting, did they all come up with different ideas? Did they find the scene more effective with or without scenery?

Chapter Two

Page 33

Choose a scene from a Shakespeare play that involves several different characters. Using a tape recorder, pretend you are making a book on tape—or even doing the voices for a new Shakespeare-based Disney animated film—and tape yourself reading the scene using a suitable voice for each character. Try to make the differentiation in characters very clear. Then, play the tape for your family and friends. Can they tell the difference between the characters? Do the different voices make it easy for them to follow the plot, or is it a distraction?

Page 46

Choose a passage from Shakespeare with which you are not familiar. Read it aloud twice to an audience: first, before you have paraphrased it, and again after. (Remember, you are paraphrasing just for your own understanding. Read the actual text to them the second time, not the paraphrase). Both times, have the audience write a summary of what the passage is about. Then, compare their summaries and discuss. Did your audience understand the passage better when **you** understood it better?

Page 53

Go through all the steps of scansion for a short verse passage of your choice. Discuss which words are more important to stress, and why. Make a markup of the passage. If necessary, compare readings out loud to decide which is better.

Chapter Three

Page 65

Act out the second half of the last scene of *Measure for Measure* in two ways: First, have Isabella accept the Duke's marriage proposal. Then, have Isabella reject the Duke's proposal. Discuss the differences. What interpretation does your audience like better? What effect does it have on the rest of the play? Which do you prefer as an actor?

Page 69

Look at a list of Shakespeare's tragedies and histories, then make up your own alternative titles for some or all of them. Try naming them more like the comedies are named, with phrases that allude to the story line. Once you have made your alternative title list, share with the others in your group. Are any of them similar? How are they different?

Page 74

Choose a Shakespeare play and try to find the actual history, myth, or story the play is based on. Choose part of the story to act out, then perform the corresponding scene of the play that is based on it. Discuss similarities and differences with your classmates. What parts of the original source did Shakespeare change? What stayed the same? What did he leave out or add in? **Variation:** Do the same exercise with a Shakespeare play and another play or story that is based on it, such as *Romeo and Juliet* and Leonard Bernstein's *West Side Story*. How does it compare to Shakespeare's story? What are the similarities and differences?

Page 79

Compare the Richards. When the great English actor, Laurence Olivier, portrayed Richard in a film way back in the 1940s, his portrayal of the king as a grotesque villain somehow became the true Richard III in everyone's mind. But another great English actor, Ian McKellen, did a film version of the play set in Nazi Germany of the 1930s. Watch both movies and discuss the actors' choices. Why do you think each chose to portray Richard the way they did? How does each performance make you feel about King Richard III? Which do you think was more effective, and why? What are the differences and similarities between the two Richards?

Page 83

Using a Shakespeare play you are familiar with, match it to its type in the Venn diagram on page 83. Then, make a list of plot points, subject matter, and characters that make the play you have chosen fall into that category. What does it have in common with other plays you know? Does your play have any characteristics that make it different from the elements listed in the category? Discuss these points with your group.

Chapter Four

Page 87

Identify modern-day character types. For each category in this chapter, list characters from modern movies, television shows, books, and plays that match the characteristics. Name two or three characters for each category. You may also want to make a list of modern characters who "break the mold"—list those that don't fit into any category, and why. Or, you can make up your own character categories that fit modern characters better. Then, compare your list to those of the rest of your group. What did you agree on? What did you disagree on, and why?

Page 100

Switch the character types and see what happens. First, choose a scene between two clear character types, such as Hamlet and Ophelia. Perform the scene as if Ophelia were a strong woman rather than an ingénue, and as if Hamlet were an evil villain. How does it affect the scene and your portrayal of the character? Do the scene three times: once changing only one character type at a time, and once changing both. **Variation:** Rewrite a character's lines to fit a different character type. Using the same example, keep Hamlet's lines the same, but rewrite Ophelia's responses as if she were a strong woman.

Page 105

Have a "villain duel." First, get a partner. Each of you chooses to portray one villain (preferably not from the same play). Pick out good phrases and lines, then create a dialogue with them. Perform your villain duel. If you want, you can have your audience vote on which villain "won" the duel. **Scene Suggestions:** Iago (from *Othello)* and Richard III (from *Richard III)*; Shylock (from *Merchant of Venice*) and Angelo (from *Measure for Measure)*. **Variation:** Do the same with a "clown duel." **Scene Suggestions:** Touchstone (from *As You Like It*) and Sir Toby Belch (from *Twelfth Night)*; Dogberry (from *Much Ado About Nothing*) and Elbow (from *Measure for Measure)*.

Chapter Five

Page 116

Write your own ending. Choose a great moment from any Shakespeare play and imagine what would have happened if that moment ended in a completely different way. Re-write the scene using your new ending and perform it for an audience. Then, perform the same scene in its original form. Ask the audience to compare the two. Which is better, and why? How would the changed scene affect the rest of the play?

Page 119

Did you notice how the dilemmas above sound like modern-day soap opera synopses? Find a synopsis from a current soap opera and use it to write your own dilemma scene from a "new" Shakespeare play. Then, cast and perform the scene. **Variation:** Take a dilemma from a Shakespeare play and put it into modern language, then perform it as if it were a scene from a soap opera.

Page 120

Divide up your kingdom. Put yourself in Lear's position and imagine that you have a kingdom to give away and three people to give it to. Then, devise a way to decide how to divide it up. Will it be an essay contest? Will you interview their friends to find out if they deserve it? Will you even tell them what they're competing for, or keep it a secret until the last minute? Write a short outline of your plan, then compare it with others'. Which is the best plan? Try acting them out and see what happens.

Page 123

Have you noticed that the hoaxes on page 123 read like sitcom plots? Take any plot from a current sitcom and write a Shakespeare-style scene based on it. Then, perform it with the other members of your group. **Variation:** Take any Shakespearean hoax and make it into a scene from a sitcom using modern language.

Page 127

Choose a modern-day dilemma, hoax, or romance. It can be something you have experienced in your own life, something from TV, the Internet, the news, or something you make up entirely. Then, write a scene from a "Shakespeare" play based on it. Perform the scene for an audience and ask them what they think.

Chapter Six

Page 132

What is the purpose of acting? Write down a list of all the reasons you think people act. Is it to entertain? Is it to get attention? Is it to express a specific viewpoint or to move the audience to action? What other reasons can you think of? Discuss your list with your group. Additionally, if you plan to become a professional actor when you grow up, think about and discuss the reasons behind your own specific career goals.

Page 133

Make a list of your favorite actors. They can be actors from movies, television, the stage, or any combination. If you want, you can list the role or roles in which each actor on your list showed his or her best attributes or did his or her best work. Take a few moments to look at the list and think about what all the actors on your list have in common. In your opinion, what makes a good actor? Then, make a list of attributes you think are important for good acting. When you are finished, compare your list with the other people in your group. Do certain names appear on some or all of the actor lists? Did you list any of the same characteristics of good acting on your attributes list? Discuss why each of you chose the actors and attributes you did. If you disagree, discuss the reasons why.

Page 141

Compare accents. If you can do a British accent, try doing a scene or monologue twice through, once using a British accent, once using your own accent. If you can't or don't feel comfortable, compare two filmed or taped versions of the same play, one British, one American. In either case, compare how the accents affect the play and the way the characters are portrayed. Which is easier to do? Which is more convincing to you?

Page 147

Do a scene or monologue with action. You will need to have it memorized. Choose an activity to do while performing your scene—it can be folding laundry, lacing and unlacing a shoe, sewing, or separating and sorting money, for example. How does this action affect your acting? Does it make it more natural? Does it affect your character's emotions? Is it easier to do it with or without the action? If possible, try performing the scene or monologue for someone twice: once with the action, once without—and compare the two.
Scene Suggestions: *Merchant of Venice,* Act II, Scene ii; *Two Gentlemen of Verona,* Act I Scene ii or Act II, Scene iii; *Richard III,* Act I, Scene i.

Page 149

Choose a monologue or scene to act out. First, do it very dramatically: Deepen your voice, draw out your words, use big, expansive gestures and loud emotions. Then, try the same scene or monologue very naturally. Which is more difficult?

Which seems more appropriate to the material? If you do it in front of an audience, which did they like better, and why? **Scene Suggestions:** *King Lear*, Act III, Scene ii; *Hamlet*, Act III, Scene iii; *Macbeth*, Act II, Scene i or ii.

Chapter Seven

Page 159

Watch the 1967 and 1996 film versions of *Romeo and Juliet* (or any other two filmed versions of one play; see Appendix B). Discuss how they compare and contrast. Some things to concentrate on are casting choices, script adaptation, setting, camera angles, speed (pace), and costumes.

Page 160

Host a Shakespearean film festival in your classroom or home (refer to Appendix B for ideas). Invite your family and/or friends. Write up expositions (or summaries of the first act) they can refer to before watching.

CLASSROOM ACTIVITIES

Chapter I

Page 7

How much do you think Shakespeare drew upon his own experiences and personality when writing his plays? Many authors, such as Ernest Hemingway, use a lot of autobiographical material when writing fiction. But other authors create characters and situations they could never have known. Just because some of Shakespeare's characters were mistrustful of religion or liked wine, does that mean he felt the same way?

Organize two groups for a debate. One group argues that Shakespeare's plays are autobiographical, using specific examples. The other group argues that the man and his art are two completely different things.

Page 8

What does it take to become a playwright, actor, or director today? We know that Shakespeare probably never went to college. If he had lived in the 21st century, would he have made it as a playwright? To learn about what kind of backgrounds today's actors, directors, and playwrights require, invite one of them to your class to discuss his or her education, training, and experience. Where did they go to school and for how long? Did they always want to have a career in the theatre? Where do they get their inspiration? If no such artists live in your area, try writing a letter to an actor, director, or playwright you admire.

Page 17

Imagine that you are the Master of Revels and that Queen Elizabeth has ordered you to plan an evening of entertainment for her and her guests. Divide the class into four groups, and put one group each in charge of plays, music, dancing, and poetry. Choose an evening or class period for your entertainment to take place. Once each group decides what they want to do, they may perform it themselves, play a recording of it (such as a film version of the play they have chosen or a recording of the music they have chosen), or ask someone else to perform it—for instance, if your school has a music department, perhaps you can find someone who plays the recorder or a group who sings madrigals; or, perhaps your town has an early music ensemble who would be willing to come play for the class or a dance teacher who can teach or perform early dances. As your evening of entertainment draws near, you may even wish to print up scrolls for those who will attend, listing what will be performed and who will be performing it. Then, sit back and enjoy!

Page 19

Many of Shakespeare's plays discuss issues that are considered controversial. In two teams, choose a controversial issue in a Shakespearean play you've read and hold a debate about it. For example: Is *The Merchant of Venice* a racist play? Does *Taming of the Shrew* have sexist overtones? With one team arguing yes and the other arguing no, debate the issue.

Page 20

Serve an Elizabethan feast. Serve any combination of roasted chicken legs and wings, boiled cabbage or other vegetables, fruit pies, meat pies, and cheese. Use bread trenchers for plates, and serve apple cider as the beverage. Eat with large spoons or with your hands. Soak up honey with bread from your trencher. Be creative with the desserts!

Page 26

Knowing all the distractions Elizabethan audiences had, how much of the plays do you think they really absorbed?

Choose any Shakespearean play on film and watch it as a class. Before you watch, assign various class members roles in the crowd: Some should be noblemen, sitting as close to the television screen as possible without blocking it, so they can see it and the rest of the class. A couple of students should be food vendors. The rest of the "crowd" should try to watch the play, but feel free to answer back to the characters if you feel so compelled, comment to your classmates when you find something interesting or disturbing, and get up to stretch or buy fruit if you want to.

Remember, though, that the point is to absorb as much of the play as you can. Afterward, answer questions on the plot and characters (your teacher can have these ready for you) and see how many you answer correctly. Discuss the experience with your classmates. Was it difficult to pay attention? Why or why not? Would you always like to see plays this way?

Chapter 2

Page 29

Choose a scene from a Shakespearean play on film (consult the list in Appendix B). Divide the class into two groups. Have one group watch the scene once. Have the other group only listen to the scene once. Then, both groups answer questions on what they remember from the scene. Compare responses and discuss which was more difficult and why. **Scene Suggestions:** *Hamlet*, Act III, Scene iv; *Twelfth Night*, Act III, Scene i.

Chapter 6

Page 136

Choose a scene that has both male and female characters in it, and then try acting it out using all boys or all girls. Then do the same scene with the proper genders playing the proper roles. How does it affect the scene? **Scene Suggestions:** *A Midsummer Night's Dream*, Act III, Scene ii; *The Merchant of Venice*, Act IV, Scene i. **Variation:** Try an all-male scene using all female actors, or vice versa. Discuss how it affects the scene. **Scene Suggestions:** *Romeo and Juliet*, Act I, Scene iii; *The Tempest*, Act II, Scene i.

LARGE GROUP ACTIVITIES

Chapter 4

Page 112

Host your own Shakespeare Awards Show. Come up with your own categories, such as "Meanest Villain," "Strongest Woman," "Most Loyal Sidekick," and "Best Speech in Iambic Pentameter." Make it as simple or complex as you like. Let everyone vote on his or her favorite Shakespearean character in each category, then announce the winners. Or if you like, you can make award statues, have people dress up as the characters to accept the awards, and even give acceptance speeches in iambic pentameter or blank verse.

Chapter 5

Page 126

What if Shakespeare's lovers appeared on a television talk show to try to work through their problems? Create your own talk show, with some of Shakespeare's famous couples—such as a modern-day Romeo and Juliet or Titania and Bottom—as the featured guests. You'll need to cast the lovers, a host, and some audience members. Remember to pick a theme: "How to say together when your families want to kill each other," or "I love my boyfriend even though he has a donkey's head." Then have the lovers explain the problem, the host ask questions and make comments, and the audience members dispense advice on how to handle star-crossed love or why Titania should kick that donkey out the door.

GLOSSARY

10-out-of-12   a rehearsal of a play, usually about a week before opening, when all the technical aspects of the production (lights, sound, costumes) are introduced for the first time. Since this often takes quite a bit of time, the company is asked to be at rehearsal for 12 hours, 10 of which are spent working and two of which are for break time.

actor   a person who performs a role on stage or film.

alliteration   the repetition of the first letter or sound of two or more words in a phrase. The phrase "a fond farewell" is alliteration with the "f" sound.

artistic liberty   the freedom that artists (such as writers, performers, and directors) take with the truth or with original material. Sometimes an artist adjusts material to make it more interesting or compelling to watch or read.

assistant stage manager   helps the stage manager carry out his duties, also acts as prompter during rehearsals. (see *stage manager*, *prompter*)

assonance   the repetition of vowel sounds in two or more words in a phrase. The phrase from *Romeo and Juliet*, "My name, dear saint, is hateful to myself" (Act II, Scene ii) repeats a long "a" sound using the words "name," "saint," and "hateful."

audience   a group of people who are in the act of watching a performance.

audition   a short trial performance in which an actor attempts to show a director what his or her abilities are, usually with the ultimate goal of being cast in a role.

aural	relating to the sense of hearing. If someone is an "aural learner," that means he or she learns best by hearing things rather than seeing or reading them.
bard	a poet and singer who composes and performs songs or poems recounting the deeds of famous heroes; a master storyteller. As a proper noun, "Bard" has come to refer specifically to William Shakespeare as a shorter term for "the Bard of Avon."
blank verse	iambic pentameter verse that does not rhyme. (see *iambic pentameter*)
blocking	an actor's movement during a play, usually decided beforehand in rehearsal.
callback	a second phase of auditions in which a select number of actors are called back to the theatre, usually to read specific roles from the script. This helps the director narrow down his or her choices for each role.
call time	the time an actor is required to be at the theatre for rehearsal or performance. In some professional theatres, actors can be fined for being late for their call time.
Catholic	before the 16th century, the Catholic Church was the only Christian church. It emphasizes sacraments (such as baptism, marriage, and communion), tradition, ordained clergy (such as priests), and good works of piety and charity.
center stage	the middle of the stage.
chain of being	the order in which Elizabethans pictured the universe. They believed everything in the universe belonged in one long chain, organized in order of importance, which began at the top with God and ended with the smallest and most insignificant things. The human part of the chain was also in a very specific order, with the queen at the top, and beggars and slaves at the bottom. Everyone in between was categorized according to the social and economic standing of the family they were born into, and it was considered going against creation and God himself to try to break out of one's place in the chain.

coat of arms	an emblem or picture denoting a specific family, handed down through the generations. The colors and objects used often have specific symbolism, such as a lion for courage or blue for loyalty. The phrase originally comes from the fact that a knight would wear a coat over his chain mail, and the coat was embroidered with the symbols describing the types of weapons ("arms") his family used.
conflict	the opposition of two characters or groups that cause the dramatic action in a play.
convention	any established theatrical practice that the audience buys into.
court dress	the style of clothing approved for wearing at a royal court.
cue line	usually the last line of an actor's speech, which is a signal to another performer that something else is to happen, such as another actor speaking, music starting, scenes changing, etc.
divine right	the belief that a monarch's right to rule a nation comes directly from God, rather than from the people they rule. This stands in stark contrast to the democratic system of government in which people can only gain leadership positions by being elected to them by the people they intend to lead.
downstage	the part of a stage closest to the audience.
dramatis personae	a list of characters in a play.
duet	a song or scene involving two people.
Elizabethan	anything from or relating to the time when Elizabeth I was the queen of England; specifically, the time period in England between 1558 and 1603.
epilogue	a section, often performed by the actor himself, at the end of a play that sums up the play's action.
falconry	the practice of breeding and training falcons and other birds of prey to hunt small animals and return to their owners.

farce a style of comedy with a far-fetched or even ridiculous plot and broad, stylized characters.

gallery a balcony with a roof in an open-air theatre in which audience members may sit to watch a play.

genre a category of artistic composition (such as plays) usually characterized by their form and content. Comedies, tragedies, histories, and romances are all examples of different genres.

groundling the informal Elizabethan term for those audience members at the Globe Theatre who stood in the pit (see *pit*) to watch the play. They were called this because the floor of the pit was literally bare ground.

headshot a photograph, usually black and white and measuring 8 inches by 10, of an actor's face. Headshots are often required at auditions so that the director is able to remember what the actor looks like afterward.

house the part of the theatre where the audience sits.

humanism a cultural system of beliefs based on the idea that good things come from people rather than (or in addition to) any supernatural deity; in Elizabethan times, this meant a return to the study of ancient Greek and Roman writings and philosophy rather than the study of the Bible or other religious texts. (see *secular*)

iambic pentameter a rhythm used in verse. Each line in iambic pentameter has five iambs. An iamb is a pair of syllables, the first unstressed, the second stressed.

imp a mischievous and sometimes evil sprite or spirit, usually found in folklore.

ingénue a character type in dramatic literature. An ingénue is an innocent, naïve girl or young woman, such as Juliet in *Romeo and Juliet* or Ophelia in *Hamlet*.

innuendo a comment, usually not complimentary, on another person's character that is not said outright but only hinted at. Innuendo is often used in comedy.

Lord Chamberlain's Men
the name of the theatre company that Shakespeare belonged to in London, consisting of ten to twelve men, called so because they were financially supported by the Lord Chamberlain.

Master of Revels
a government officer appointed by Queen Elizabeth I whose responsibilities were to oversee and regulate the business of theatre companies. These duties included the censorship and licensing of all plays, the arrangements for theatre companies to perform at court for the queen, and the approval of theatre companies to be formed and to perform regularly.

monologue
a speech, usually part of a play, that is performed by only one actor. Monologues are usually required at auditions as a sample of an actor's ability.

movie
an interpretation of a story using motion picture.

off-book
a term used when an actor has memorized a script well enough that he or she no longer needs to look at it. During a rehearsal process, there is usually a deadline when all actors must be off-book. For a short period of time after that, actors can still be prompted by the assistant stage manager if they forget a line.

onomatopoetic
when words sound like what they mean, or imitate the sound of the item they describe, such as "boom" or "whoosh." Shakespeare frequently uses onomatopoeia.

open-air theatre
a theatre that is not enclosed, so as to let in as much natural light as possible. In Elizabethan theatres, the stage and the galleries (see *gallery*) had roofs over them, but the center of the structure, called the pit (see *pit*), was open to the sky.

period costume
costumes designed to look like what was worn during a specific period, that is, a specific time in history. For instance, period costumes for the American 1960s would look like what people typically wore in America in the '60s.

pit
the middle of a circular outdoor theatre such as the Globe. The pit was a flat, dirt floor on which audience members could stand to watch the play. The stage jutted out into the

pit and was roughly five feet above its surface, so those standing in the pit would be looking up at the players.

pilgrimage a religious person's journey to a special and meaningful shrine or sacred place.

plague an outbreak of infectious disease with a high death rate; in Elizabethan England, this meant the Bubonic Plague, which killed thousands at the turn of the 17th century.

player one of the actors in a play.

preview an early performance, often a final dress rehearsal, to which audience members are invited, often for a reduced ticket price.

prologue an introduction or preface to a play, poem, book, etc.

prompter the person in an Elizabethan theatre company who was in charge of making sure all actors had their scripts or sides (see *side*) and who would aid in rehearsals by following the script and providing words if actors forgot their lines. The prompter was also in charge of running performances (similar to a modern-day stage manager) and of keeping track of what costumes, props, and music were needed for each play.

prop short for "property." Any object that is used in the performance of the play that is not painted scenery or costume. Props include everything from furniture to knickknacks to anything the characters might use, such as weapons or food.

prose ordinary language in which people write and speak, as opposed to poetic verse.

protagonist usually the main character in a play, who drives the action, or around whom the action is centered.

Protestant a person or Church that is Christian but not Catholic, and who denies that the Pope has authority over all Christians. Also, Protestants believe they can be forgiven for their sins without the aid of a priest (or member of the clergy). The Protestant Church was formed in the

	mid-1500s and was solidified as the Church of England during Queen Elizabeth I's reign.
pun	a joke made by using the play of similar words or sounds.
read-through	often the first rehearsal of a play, at which all the actors sit down to read the play out loud.
realistic	a style of acting that strives to be more believable and natural and less dramatic, artificial, and overdone.
repertoire	a number of plays that a single theatre company is able to perform at any time.
resolution	in a play, the point at which the main problem is worked out.
resume	a one-page summary of an actor's talents, skills, education, and experience. A resume also includes the actor's major physical attributes (height, weight, hair color, etc.) and contact information. Resumes are often printed on the back of an actor's headshot.
rhyme	words with the same ending sound, most often in the ends of lines of verse.
ritual	an act or series of acts repeatedly performed according to a specific custom.
romance	a literary genre characterized by adventurous plots, characters, and settings.
satire	a type of comedy that makes fun of human mistakes using sarcasm and stereotypes.
scansion	the analysis of poetic verse.
secular	philosophy, literature, art, or music that is not religious or spiritual in nature or subject matter; having nothing to do with any spiritual deity; of or having to do with the world as opposed to heaven.
side	a booklet or scroll containing a single character's cues and lines from a play.

slang
an informal vocabulary made up of non-standard word usage and invented words. Although sometimes slang ends up in standard English, most slang does not last very long.

slapstick
a type of comedy focused on silly, clumsy, physical humor. When we laugh at people falling down or running into doors, we are laughing at slapstick.

soliloquy
a set of lines spoken by a character by himself onstage, as if talking to himself or the audience.

stage directions
the vocabulary used to explain locations on a stage, usually for blocking purposes. Stage directions are usually given from the point of view of the actor facing the audience.

stage left
the left part of a stage, as the actor faces the audience.

stage manager
a person in charge of making sure a production runs smoothly. A stage manager records blocking and prompts actors in rehearsals, organizes the rehearsal process, and organizes all of the technical aspects during the show (such as giving the order for a scene change or lighting change).

stage right
the right part of a stage, as the actor faces the audience.

Stanislavski, Konstantin
(1863–1938) a Russian actor, director, and teacher, Stanislavski revolutionized acting technique by creating a more simplistic yet intensely psychological style of acting. He laid the groundwork for what eventually became Method Acting in America. He also founded the Moscow Art Theatre.

subjective
when reality or truth is perceived by an individual and their opinion, as opposed to being a universal truth that everyone agrees upon. Acting is a subjective art, meaning that just because one person perceives it to be good does not make that a universal truth.

subplot
a secondary plot in a play or book.

table work	text work done by a cast around a table, usually in rehearsals prior to blocking.
technique	any method of acting.
tetralogy	a set of four literary works (such as plays) whose stories run in succession. It is similar to a trilogy, but includes one more.
theatre	a building (or outdoor structure) in which the live representation of an action or story takes place.
thrust	a stage surrounded by the audience on three sides; the fourth side is a wall with doors leading into the backstage area, through which actors can make their entrances and exits.
tragedy	a genre of plays characterized by the protagonist's unsuccessful struggle against forces beyond his or her control, which usually end in death or disaster.
unities	dramatic rules, originating from the Greek writer Aristotle, that require that a play should concern a single action and should take place in one setting on one day. These are called the unities of action, place, and time.
upstage	the part of the stage farthest from the audience.
viewer	one who watches a performance.
visceral	something so compelling as to be felt with the whole body.
yard	(see *pit*)

APPENDIX E

WORKS CONSULTED

Books Consulted

Abrams, M. H. (Ed.). (1993). *The Norton Anthology of English Literature.* (6th Ed., Vol. 1). New York: W. W. Norton and Company.

Barton, J. (1984). *Playing Shakespeare: An Actor's Guide.* New York: Anchor Books.

Barton, R. (1993). *Style for Actors.* Mountain View, CA: Mayfield Publishing Company.

Bloom, H. (1998). *Shakespeare: The Invention of the Human.* New York: Riverhead Books.

Brockett, O. G. (1991). *History of the Theatre.* (6th Ed.). Boston: Allyn and Bacon.

Claybourne, A. and Treays, R. (1996). *The World of Shakespeare.* London: Usborne Publishing.

Doyle, J. & Lischner, R. (1999). *Shakespeare for Dummies.* Hoboken: Wiley.

Gurr, A. (1996). *Playgoing in Shakespeare's London.* (2nd Ed.). Cambridge: Cambridge University Press.

Holden, A. (1999). *William Shakespeare: The Man Behind the Genius.* Boston: Little, Brown and Company.

James, J. & Morley, J. (1998). *Shakespeare's Theatre.* East Sussex, England: Macdonald Young Books.

Lamb, S., (Ed.) (2000). *Cliffs Complete Shakespeare's Hamlet.* Hoboken: Wiley.

LoMonico, M. (2001). *The Shakespeare Book of Lists.* Franklin Lakes, NJ: New Page Books.

McQuain, J. & Malless, S. (1998). *Coined by Shakespeare: Words and Meanings First Penned by the Bard.* Springfield, MA: Merriam-Webster, Inc.

Mowat, B. A., & Werstine, P. (Eds.). (1992–1994). *The New Folger Library Shakespeare* (All vols.). New York: Washington Square Press.

O'Brien, P. (1993). *Shakespeare Set Free: Teaching* Romeo and Juliet, Macbeth, *and* A Midsummer Night's Dream. New York: Washington Square Press.

Onions, C. T. (Ed.). (1986). *A Shakespeare Glossary.* Oxford: Oxford University Press.

Packard, W., Pickering, D., & Savidge, C. (Eds.). (1988). *The Facts on File Dictionary of the Theatre.* New York: Facts on File.

Pritchard, R. E., Ed. (2000). *Shakespeare's England: Life in Elizabethan and Jacobean Times.* Phoenix Mill, England: Sutton Publishing.

Pritner, C. & Colaianni, L. (2001). *How to Speak Shakespeare.* Santa Monica: Santa Monica Press.

Schmidt, A. (Ed.). (1902). *Shakespeare Lexicon and Quotation Dictionary* (3rd ed., Vols 1–2). New York: Dover Publications, Inc.

Sobran, J. (1997). *Alias Shakespeare: Solving the Greatest Literary Mystery of All Time.* New York: The Free Press.

Tillyard, E. M. W. (1959). *The Elizabethan World Picture.* New York: Vintage Books.

Tucker, P. (2002). *Secrets of Acting Shakespeare: The Original Approach.* New York: Routledge.

Weir, A. (1998). *The Life of Elizabeth I.* New York: Ballantine Publishing Group.

Wells, Stanley. (1995). *Shakespeare: A Life in Drama.* New York: W. W. Norton and Company.

Wright, W. A. (Ed.). (1936). *The Complete Works of William Shakespeare: The Cambridge Edition Text.* Garden City, NY: Garden City Books.

Websites Consulted

15 Ancient Greek Heroes from Plutarch's *Lives.* www.e-classics.com/index.html

Amleth, Prince of Denmark. www.pitt.edu/~dash/amleth.html

The Geoffrey Chaucer Page: *The Canterbury Tales.* http://icg.fas.harvard.edu/~chaucer/cantales.html

Life in Elizabethan England: A Compendium of Common Knowledge. http://renaissance.dm.net/compendium/

Merriam-Webster Online. www.m-w.com

Metamorphoses by Ovid. http://classics.mit.edu/Ovid/metam.html

Mr. William Shakespeare and the Internet.
    http://shakespeare.palomar.edu/default.htm

Puck through the Ages: The History of a Hobgoblin.
    www.geocities.com/Athens/Acropolis/4198/puckages.html

Renascence Editions: An Online Repository of Works Printed in English
    Between the Years 1477 and 1799.
    www.shu.ac.uk/emls/iemls/resour/mirrors/rbear/ren.htm

Richard III Society, American Branch. www.r3.org

Shakespeare and the Globe: Then and Now.
    http://www.britannica.com/shakespeare/ind_bios.html

Shakespeare Online. www.shakespeare-online.com

NOTES

❦ NOTES ❦

❦ NOTES ❦

❦ NOTES ❦

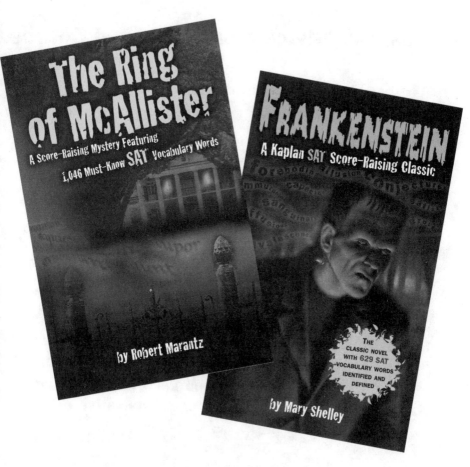

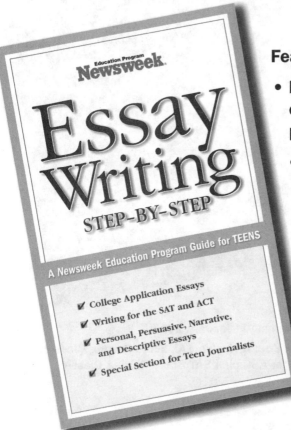